FOR A BETTER CONGRESS:

Fifty Questions Your Congressman Should Answer If They Want Your Vote

Steven B. Larchuk
Kathleen B. Entenmann

"The mismanagement of our economy and the mismanagement of globalization are, in turn, related to the role of special interests in our politics - a politics that increasingly represents the 1 percent. But while politics has been part of the cause of our current troubles, it will only be through reform of our democracy - making our government more accountable to all of the people, more reflective of their interests -that we will be able to heal the great divide and restore the country to shared prosperity."

Joseph E. Stiglitz, PhD, Winner of the Nobel Prize. From his book, *The Great Divide: Unequal Societies and What We Can Do About Them.*

****

DEDICATION

This book is dedicated to the goal of a Better Congress for our children, and for yours.

****

HOW TO USE THIS BOOK

Every two years the American People have the opportunity to reinvent their government by simply electing a new Congress. All 435 seats of the House of Representatives and one third of the Senate are at stake. Given the importance of Congress you would think many qualified citizens would seek election, but few actually do. And most of those who do run are insufficiently tested.

An all too common campaign tactic is to avoid answering voter questions. Pivot. Say what you came to say rather than discuss an awkward topic. Better to look rude by ignoring the question than to answer it and in the process depart from carefully crafted talking points. It is also considered a rookie mistake to state any position that has not been focus group tested.

As voters we routinely let candidates get away with this. They finesse rather than answer the hard questions which define our times. We have been unwilling to demand answers and accountability, and as a result we have the Congress we deserve. Time for that to change. We need a better Congress.

Here is a collection of fifty suggested questions for candidates to Congress. They are grouped into seven general areas of concern: *The Economy,*

National Security, Health Care and Elder Care, Our Environment, Privacy and Personal Liberty, Education, and Governance.

Of course there are hundreds more very good questions that should also be asked, but this is a start. In addition to suggesting these questions we also offer proposed answers. These responses are sometimes as short as a single word. Others require a few sentences. But the goal is always candor and brevity.

After each response are suggestions for action by a Better Congress. "A Better Congress Will ..."

For those voters looking for more depth there is also a "Discussion" of each topic, again sometimes short and other times going on a bit.

It is not expected or even desired that the reader will agree with all of the proposed answers or the analysis. The purpose of this book is to stimulate the dialog between the candidate and the voter which has been too long absent from American politics. Democracy cannot be a spectator sport. We all need to work harder, For a Better Congress.

FOR A BETTER CONGRESS

Introduction

ARTICLE SEVEN - PAGE 251
GOVERNANCE

Majority Rule. Can Congress Handle It?

Is Money Really Speech?

Should There Be Congressional Term Limits?

Voter identification –
Necessary Safeguard of Democracy
Or Calculated Voter Suppression?

What Constitutional Amendments Would You Support?

What Will You Do After You Leave Congress?

Immigration Reform – How Will You Vote?

Bonus Question –
Can One Congressman Make a Difference?

****

Acknowledgments – Page 284

****

FOR A BETTER CONGRESS

INTRODUCTION

When the framers of the Constitution did their work they did so in just under four months and with remarkable brevity. A Preamble and Seven Articles covering four handwritten pages composed the entire foundation of a completely new and original national government, coexisting and sharing sovereignty with the States. Within the next two years, the Constitution was ratified and the first Ten Amendments were adopted for the purpose of making it even clearer that our government, unlike any other government in the World, is premised on the bedrock principle that all power resides in and originates from the People.

Having risked everything to gain their Liberty from an oppressive monarch, the People of the United States wanted to reaffirm that their new Federal government would have only the authority granted it by the Constitution exercised by elected representatives acting within the limits of their authority as defined by that Constitution.

That remarkable document begins with what we would recognize today as a mission statement:

We the People of the United States, in Order to form a more perfect Union, establish Justice, insure domestic Tranquility, provide for the common defense, promote the general Welfare, and secure the Blessings of Liberty to ourselves and to our Posterity, do ordain and establish this Constitution for the United States of America.

"We the People." Upon these three simple words all that has followed in the centuries since has depended. Government, resting upon the wisdom and shoulders of its citizens. Lately some political groups have hijacked these words, laying the exclusive claim to be "We the People." They are not the first to do so, nor will they be the last.

Parsing the Preamble out a bit further, other key words are: union, justice, tranquility, defense, general welfare, liberty, and our posterity. If we were rewriting the Preamble today we would likely add freedom, equality and privacy, but otherwise the original stands up remarkably well after over two hundred years of wear and tear.

Our Constitution survived the Civil War, during the midst of which Abraham Lincoln observed that our "new Nation" had been "conceived in liberty, and dedicated to the proposition that all men are created equal." By so saying Lincoln was reaching back even before the Constitution, to the Declaration of Independence, as a preamble to the Preamble. As he continued his remarks at Gettysburg, Lincoln described the horrors of the Civil War as a test, "whether that Nation, or any nation so conceived and so dedicated can long endure?"

What Lincoln did not say, and what is only implied in the Declaration of Independence, Constitution, and all of the 27 Amendments since, is that our American experiment is built on trust and character. Trust that those with differing opinions or interests will conduct themselves ethically and with honor. Character such that each of us will restrain ourselves from taking unfair advantage of imperfections in our laws or the inevitable, but transitory, imbalances in numbers or wealth.

Parchment and speeches, no matter how inspiring or poetic, are no substitute for trust and character. In every American political crisis the seeds of discord can be found months, often years, earlier when it becomes clear that the disputing sides have lost confidence in each other, or the side with the advantage is exceeding the unmarked boundaries of civility in favor of exploiting their edge to achieve a disproportionate gain. In such times we also find that our courts sometimes fail their responsibility as an honest broker.

In the 21st Century we are again experiencing a test of whether our Nation can long endure. While there are no great armies marching in blue and gray, we have two factions that have been sometimes labeled as the one percent and the ninety-nine percent. Less precisely, but more accurately, the issue is wealth disparity and the abuse of that wealth by some to control the economy and national governance.

According to the U.S. Census Bureau, 40% of the wealth of this Country is concentrated in the hands of just 1% of its citizens. This is not unprecedented; wealth disparity was at about this same level in 1928, on the eve of the Great Depression. But now is the first time in a century that the wealthy have so shamelessly abused their financial advantage to cross the line and cynically disregard the essential balance of trust and character. Without that balance the Nation is drifting toward a new feudalism where overwhelming political and economic power resides in the hands of a privileged few while the rest fight over what remains.

Not all those of wealth are guilty of this misconduct, but too many are. Throughout this book those who are determined to stop at nothing to achieve complete control are sometimes referred to as the Insatiable Wealthy. There is no limit to their hunger for wealth and power and so they are, in fact, insatiable.

Fortunately, what has been referred to by some as a "vast right wing conspiracy" is actually not so vast. A remarkably small number control the wealth of this Nation. However, they project and leverage their power through the use and control of the media and by funding the campaigns of compliant candidates.

In the late 1800's and early 1900's we saw this same phenomenon with the growth of financial behemoths and corporate combinations, so-called "trusts," that dominated every major industry and the financial system. They were opposed by the populists of the day who called upon the native independent spirit of Americans to resist the relentless influence of concentrated wealth.

Was it not for the historical accident of Theodore Roosevelt's progressive presidency and overwhelming popularity the dominance of the trusts may have continued. Instead we saw the passage of "Antitrust" laws aimed at breaking up such monopolies. At the same time there evolved a union movement and laws passed as part of Franklin Roosevelt's "New Deal" that protected labor's right to organize. The Federal income tax was made possible by adoption of the 16th Amendment and its graduated tax rates helped to slow the accumulation of economic power, as did the adoption of estate taxes. For decades these measures tempered the concentration of wealth and helped restore and sustain the vital balance of power that had been threatened.

We survived the Depression, a World War and a Cold War, and most shared in the National prosperity.

By contrast, today, we again find our Nation out of balance and at risk. The difference is that this time the wealthy have succeeded through clever marketing and extravagant spending to persuade a large percentage of Americans that it is in their best interest to allow the wealth to accumulate in the hands of a few. The popular will that had enabled a Teddy Roosevelt and his cousin, Franklin, to press Congress toward reform has instead been warped and distracted with the assistance of a stubborn core of well-paid media advocates for the interests of the wealthy over the rest of the Country.

It is hard now to remember that with its losses in 2006 and 2008 the old Republican Party was so defeated that some wondered if it could survive as an organized political force. It was a franchise flat on its back and ripe to be overtaken by an alliance between extreme social and financial conservatives.

By 2014, this coalition of extreme socially conservative Republicans (anti-gay, anti-union, anti-immigrant, anti-women, anti-environment, anti-health care reform) and government hating "Tea Party" candidates (all government is bad), with the financial and media support of the Insatiable Wealthy, purged all moderate Republicans and managed to gain control of both houses of Congress.

This has been by design, not accident, and those who have been handed power by the wealthy are loath to betray their masters. Step by step all of the measures adopted to establish a balance in the early 1900's and in response to the Depression have come under attack.

If anyone doubts this they need look no further for an example than the vote of the House of Representatives on April 15, 2015. Throughout the 2014 House and Senate races the Republican/Tea Party candidates promised tax reform for all. Those who bought into this promise likely thought that it meant some sort of relief generally for the working people of America. After all, the Tea Party movement was founded on the acronym "Taxed Enough Already".

So it was likely a shock to those who voted for tax reform to learn that the Republican/Tea Party plan was limited to a complete repeal of the estate tax. This is the tax that only impacts estates in excess of $5 Million – in other words it affects just two-tenths of one percent of Americans. Put another way, this so-called tax reform meant nothing to 99.8% of the American public. The trick, and it is just that, has been to rebrand the estate tax as the dreaded "Death Tax". And, in fact, on that symbolic April 15th, instead of tax reform for all Americans the Republican/Tea Party coalition passed, "The Death Tax Elimination Act of 2015".

Although we could have wished otherwise, our Supreme Court is simply an enabler in all of this. With its hand picking of the President in 2000 and the *Citizens United* decision overturning the bipartisan election reforms that had imperfectly checked the power of money in American politics, the Supreme Court has forfeited any pretense of neutrality. Instead, the conservative majority of the Justices have allowed the politics of their appointment to control their decisions.

With the loss of character and self-restraint by those who have gained near total power, the fundamental requirement of trust has also been lost, and with it the invisible but essential glue that has held our Country together. What remains is the question whether that loss of trust is something from which we can recover. Can this Nation, so conceived and so dedicated, endure this new civil war?

If it can, and if it will, the responsibility rests where it has since the beginning, with the People. Certainly the election of competent and compassionate presidents in 2016 and thereafter is essential. However, to truly recover we must elect a Better Congress. And a Better Congress begins with the election of better representatives and senators.

Every two years Americans have the opportunity to renew their political marriage vows. With revitalized trust and character and from every corner of America we must get our noses out of our cell phones and engage in the process that calls for our mature attention and participation. It also requires our collective ability to ignore the bombast of political cable networks, biased newspapers, and talk radio entertainers.

We need to recognize political advertising for the fraud that it is – proof only of who has the greater access to funding and the bias of the media ownership.

"For a Better Congress" is more than just the title of a book. It is a challenge that every generation of Americans must face sooner or later. Now is our time.

ARTICLE ONE

THE ECONOMY

The Questions:

Can the United States Bounce a Check?

Does It Matter That 40% of America's Wealth Is Controlled by the Top 1%?

Infrastructure Investment – Why Wait?
How Can We Rebuild the Middle Class?

Do You Support Collective Bargaining?

Is There Too Much Bank Deregulation?

International Trade Treaties – Essential or Oversold?

"Whoever controls the volume of money in Any country is absolute master of all Industry and commerce."

James A. Garfield

****

QUESTION:

Can The United States Bounce A Check?

Answer: Only if it wants to.

****

A Better Congress Will:

> ➢ Appreciate that Congress cannot cut, save or tax its way to a healthier economy.

> ➢ Understand that as a sovereign nation the United States controls its own monetary policy and can use the Federal Reserve to fund an Infrastructure Bank and similar public banks to jump start a resurgence of the Middle Class.

> ➢ Take a lesson from our recent experiences with Quantitative Easing and realize that progressive monetary policy is long overdue and must be better targeted to the Middle Class.

> ➢ Pass enabling legislation to allow and encourage the Federal Reserve to address the existing monetary famine which is killing the American Middle Class.

****

Discussion:

Next time a politician rants about a balanced budget ask them whether the United States can bounce a check? If they do not understand the question, or answer "yes", you need to find another candidate.

We learned a few things during the Great Recession. One of them was that the Federal Reserve has the power to inject trillions of dollars into our economy without triggering inflation or forcing an international devaluation of the dollar. In doing so the Federal Reserve proved, again, that the United States cannot bounce a check. That, and much more.

As a sovereign power the United States has the ability, and responsibility, to increase the money supply as needed. This is done through a few computer keystrokes at the Federal Reserve.

It is also the Federal Reserve that essentially honors the financial obligations of the United States. This means that it is not possible for the United States to default on a debt or issue checks that will not be paid by the Federal Reserve when presented. All obligations of the United States incurred under laws passed by Congress and signed by the President will be honored regardless of the amount of tax revenue.

This is all possible because, in 1971, the United States went off the gold standard. This meant the amount of dollars in circulation would no longer be limited by the amount of gold we physically possessed. Instead, the Federal Reserve can manipulate the supply of dollars at its discretion.

Small business and consumers require sufficient general liquidity, meaning sufficient dollars in circulation. This is just as a body needs enough blood and that blood has to circulate to do its work. Unfortunately, for too long the Federal Reserve has weighed the health of Main Street as a secondary consideration to the well-being of the huge financial institutions operating out of New York, London, Tokyo and elsewhere. And these major international banks fear inflation above all else.

As a result the Federal Reserve has been timid. Over the past two generations, in its caution to avoid inflation it has allowed a monetary famine to afflict the economy to the extreme detriment of the Middle Class.

Yes, every so often, and to exaggerated media fanfare, the Federal Reserve has allowed a little more or less liquidity depending upon its analysis of the health of the economy and the rate of inflation. Initially this was the same strategy used during the early days of the recent Recession. That changed when all of the tweaking mechanisms that had been employed over the years to expand or contract the money supply proved inadequate to address the international financial crisis brought on by those very banks the Federal Reserve had worked so hard to protect and nourish.

Instead of the usual pinch of digital dollars salt here and there, the Federal Reserve ultimately had no choice but to finally use its authority to create trillions of dollars from thin air to cover the Federal deficits created during the Recession. Ill understood then, and hotly debated since, it was a Hail Mary pass. Desperate times calling for seemingly desperate measures.

Naturally this caused substantial anxiety among the deficit hawks who refused to acknowledge that the United States is not like a household, a small business, or even a state - none of which have the ability to create money. The usual balanced books accounting rules simply do not apply to the United States any more than they apply to the UK, Japan, Australia, The People's Republic of China or any other sovereign nation that has retained the power to control its own money supply.

This is not printing paper money. It is much more than that and in fantastically large amounts. This is digital money. Remember, since 1971 there has not even been the suggestion that American dollars are backed by gold or anything else tangible.

So what stands behind the dollar? Faith. Nothing more, but nothing less either.

Reviewing the history again is essential. In the darkest days of the financial crisis of 2008, Congress followed the recommendations of President Bush, and then in 2009 President Obama, to pass historic tax reduction and public spending legislation which required deficits at undreamed of levels. The conventional wisdom at the time was that the cost of Federal borrowing from domestic and International sources, would bankrupt America while simultaneously draining every available dollar from the World economy, thus making it impossible for businesses and individuals to borrow to meet day to day business needs. This was an abyss that threatened to destroy the international economy as we understood it.

Such fears were based upon the belief that there is a limited amount of money and that government books must balance. Neither belief is true. Although balancing your books as an individual or business is virtuous and necessary, this is not the case with a sovereign nation such as the United States. As economist Warren Mosler has written, the Federal Reserve can no more run out of dollars than a football field can run out of points.

So the Federal Reserve threw its Hail Mary in the form of massive infusions of digital dollars into the economy. In essence the United States financed its deficit this way. From thin air. It was called Quantitative Easing, and as a result the United States Treasury did not have to borrow from others, international liquidity was preserved, and those dollars instead remained in the economy to keep interest rates low and to assure enough financial blood to eventually, at least partially, re-prime the pump of the economy.

At the time Quantitative Easing was seen by many as reckless. The deficit hawks, economic anarchists really, who would have preferred to see the Country utterly fail rather than tinker with the sacred dollar, were enraged and issued dire warnings that the economy would collapse and we would all need a wheelbarrow to carry enough money to the store to purchase a loaf of bread. One can imagine the collective holding of breath in Washington D.C. and New York.

And yet, there was no great inflation. To the contrary inflation dropped to historically low levels. There was no weakening of the dollar against foreign currency. Rather, the value of the dollar has risen dramatically, 50% against the Yen for example. International banks and governments have mildly complained but the strength of the American economy is essential to the recovery of our trading partners and therefore, they have taken no action.

To the contrary, instead they too have initiated Quantitative Easing programs of their own since austerity only made their recessions deeper and longer. In truth the teetering and near collapse of Greece is the clearest example of the folly of more austerity when the opposite medicine is what is really required.

In short, we tried an experiment in a crisis. It worked. We survived. And in the process we proved what should have been obvious from the start. Quantitative Easing is an available and powerful tool.

So, the United States cannot bounce a check. Unless it wants to. And why would we ever want to?

Authors' Note: Many thanks to economist Warren Mosler who originally provided the answer, "only if it wants to" in response to the Co-Author's question, "Can the United States bounce a check"? Understanding the question, and the answer, is a litmus test for the qualification of any Congressman to discuss monetary policy.

*"We can go through the list over and over,
But at the end of every line is this:
Republicans believe this country should
Work for those who are rich, those who are
Powerful, those who can hire armies of
Lobbyists and lawyers, I will tell you we can
Whimper about it, we can whine about it,
Or we can fight back."*

Senator Elizabeth Warren

*"There's class warfare, all right, but it's my
class, the rich class, that's making war, and
we're winning."*

Warren Buffett

****

QUESTION:

*Does It Matter That 40% of America's Wealth Is
Controlled by the Top 1%?*

Answer: Yes, it is a threat to the fundamental
stability and legitimacy of our society.

****

A Better Congress Will:

> ➤ Increase the Minimum Wage to a Living
>   Wage Indexed to inflation.

> ➤ Strengthen Laws Protecting Collective
>   Bargaining.

> Limit Campaign Contributions and Require Full Disclosure On Political Speech.

> Maintain the Estate Tax Where It Is and Eliminate Loopholes.

> Restore Capital Gains and Dividend Tax Rates to 1998 Levels.

> Impose a Transaction Fee On All Securities Transactions.

> Lift Caps on Eligible Social Security and Medicare Taxable Income.

****

Discussion:

Those most distressed by the state of our Country sometimes become nostalgic and long for a return to simpler days following World War II when the economy boomed, jobs were plentiful, and the Middle Class expanded such that there was a great demand for vehicles and new houses. It was also an era when the prosperity was shared and the gaps between the economic classes were relatively narrow.

And then, at about 1980, the distance between the top income earners and everyone else began to grow. What happened? What is clear is that since 1980, at least, the gains in income (adjusted for inflation) have been concentrated at the top while the typical working American has been working harder but essentially treading water. Beginning with the Reagan Administration the gap has steadily widened. It is not just an expression that the "rich keep getting richer," it is a fact. This trend is also mirrored by a shocking and expanding wealth disparity.

As one researches the question of the widening gap between the wealthy and the rest of the population you find dozens of books, studies and reports that may differ on the fine detail, but not in their essential and shared conclusion. The wealth of the United States is becoming concentrated in the hands of a financial aristocracy. The last time it was this severe was on the eve of the Great Depression, 1928.

At the same time the ability of the average working American to get ahead, or even keep up, has ended. Wages for working people have been essentially frozen for close to forty years.

What is so remarkable is that there really is no debate about the facts and the likely trends. Nor do the wealthy seriously claim this is a healthy situation. Sure, there is the occasional nonsensical claim that the wealthy are the "job creators". Of course, the People as a whole are the consumers of substantially all goods and services and thus it is the average American who is the job creator. The wealthy can only drive so many cars, consume so many steaks, live in so many houses. They do not spread the wealth. There is no trickle down. Once capital is in the top tier it tends to stay there. Monetary hoarding.

In a society that is held together by the shared belief that the deck is not stacked and that with hard work anyone can rise and share in the wealth of America, the reality is a punch to the collective gut. It is unreasonable to expect a nation established on the fundamental belief that all men are created equal to tolerate this much longer.

Certainly the wealthy recognize the injustice of the situation. A laudable number, the Enlightened Wealthy, are gifting sizeable shares of their money to charities of all sorts. In many cases their targeted giving makes the difference where government priorities create gaps.

Understanding that for decades the largest percentage of Americans have either stayed in place or lost wealth also means there has been an accumulating and compounding wealth deficit year after year. As noted, the rich can only consume so much. Therefore, in the process of the rich accumulating, but not spending, the wealth of the nation has become bottled up. Stranded. Leading to the phenomenon of a monetary famine afflicting the 99%.

Money is like blood: it has to circulate to do its work. This is the essential concept, and the Middle Class has bled out.

Historically one tool to restore the balance has been a heavy estate tax. Inevitably the wealthy would pass away and a substantial portion of their estates would be paid over to the Federal Government where it would be expended on various government programs while reducing the need to raise tax money from the less well off. State governments also took a slice with similar economic impact at the local level. Some call this a wealth transfer – it is really a wealth restoration to the working classes from which all production and wealth is created. In this way the wealth at the top came back into the general economy – a transfusion.

Over the past decades a highly successful campaign from conservatives to reduce, and eventually end, the estate tax gained a boost when the levy was cleverly branded as the "death tax" and cynically and inaccurately associated with the break-up of such all American favorites as family farms and small family owned businesses.

Over time, incrementally, the estate tax impact has been reduced to the point that by 2015 only estates in excess of $5 Million are subject to the tax. This is effectively a partial repeal.

This also means that 99.8% of Americans have no exposure whatsoever to the dreaded death tax – and yet the Republican/Tea Party coalition of Congress makes an annual show of voting to eliminate the estate tax altogether in the name of "tax reform".

Tax rates on those with higher incomes have also been reduced over time resulting in less tax revenue despite higher incomes. With such reductions of income tax rates on high earners, reduced capital gains taxes, and partial repeal of the estate tax – automatic restoration of the necessary social economic balance by harvesting money from the top is no longer happening. Nor is it likely to happen again so long as disproportionate wealth translates into overwhelming political influence.

Many progressives shake their fist and demand higher taxes on the rich as the path toward financing social programs and restoring balance. That is howling at the moon. Unless the Insatiable

Wealthy have a sudden, and unlikely, change of heart they will continue to use their wealth to support politicians from dog catcher to president who will protect and preserve the unique status of this American oligarchy.

As discussed elsewhere, the better strategy is to use the power of the Federal Reserve to increase the money supply through targeted infusions into the Middle Class and in this fashion replace the liquidity that has been bottled up at the top. This does not stick a finger in the eye of the wealthy as it does not take from them that which they are unwilling to give.

As Benjamin Franklin famously declared, "politics is the art of the possible" – and attempting to reform and revive our economy with a barricades and pitchfork militancy is not possible. There is a better path and a Better Congress will follow it.

"We need to stop thinking about Infrastructure as an economic stimulant and Start thinking about it as a strategy. Economic stimulants produce Bridges to Nowhere. Strategic investment in Infrastructure produces a foundation for Long-term growth."

Roger McNamee

****

QUESTION:

Infrastructure Investment – Why Wait?

Answer: We should not wait. Extensive investment in modern transportation, housing, clean water, sustainable energy, health care facilities, and education infrastructure will inject much needed income into the pockets of Middle Class America while strengthening American competitiveness.

****

A Better Congress Will:

➢ Establish an Infrastructure Bank that will provide the funds needed to launch and maintain the rebuilding and advancement of key American assets. This will also generate the well compensated jobs we need to rebuild the Middle Class.

➢ Direct the Federal Reserve to provide all necessary funding and liquidity to support these projects as part of its existing job creating mandate.

> ➤ Require importers of steel and other materials to certify that any non-USA source is in full compliance with all trade policies that require a level playing field with respect to labor standards and environmental considerations.

****

Discussion:

In her recent book, *Move – Putting America's Infrastructure Back in the Lead*, Dr. Rosabeth Moss Kanter, provides an inspiring and exciting vision of better, faster, safer, and more efficient United States transportation for freight and passengers, whether the trip is across town or across the Continent. She also advocates substantial investment in our cities and communication infrastructure as a means of revitalizing the economy and vaulting the United States back into the lead.

Along the way Dr. Kantor risks committing the sin of bruising American pride by pointing out that when it comes to modern infrastructure the United States is well behind many other nations. Yet she never fails to remind her readers that we have been the innovators of nearly all of the systems we have allowed to decay, and we have the ability to resume our leadership if we can just find the will - and the money.

Ah yes, the money. And so, after telling us the "what" Dr. Kanter joins the chorus and advocates an infrastructure bank: and that is the "how". She notes that other countries have successfully established such institutions to finance their large projects. Some in Congress are already working on it.

For example, in May 2015, Republican Senator Deb Fischer of Nebraska offered her "Build USA Act" intended to help States borrow infrastructure funding at lower interest rates. Unfortunately, Senator Fischer proposes to capitalize her version of the Infrastructure Bank through the return by the States of unused allocations of previous Federal grants. We must do better than that.

This is difficult as we currently suffer a Congress obsessed with shrinking the size of government and reducing taxes. It is a maddening teeth pulling exercise to even achieve modest increases and reauthorizations of the Highway Trust Fund. Hard core deficit hawks refuse to allow necessary increases in the fuel tax to cover the lost revenue from lower gasoline sales.

Recognizing this, Dr. Kanter twists and turns in the later chapters of her book through different public-private financing mechanisms and looks for pots of potential money in the private sector. Ultimately she comes up empty despite flirting with the answer.

In fact the solution is right in front of us. By definition an infrastructure bank loans various governments, or even the private businesses, the funds to build very large institutional projects and takes a lien on the resulting assets. In other words these are collateralized loans. The projects are collateral for the money to build them. Unfortunately, when the money comes from the private sector, it removes billions of dollars from the pool of capital available to fund competing day-to-day business operations and other private sector projects. This results in a higher cost of borrowing as businesses are forced to fight over what is left after governments have had their fill. Ordinary commercial borrowing also becomes more difficult as the underwriting standards and qualifications for borrowers are tightened, thus disqualifying marginal businesses or start-ups and stifling growth.

So why go to the private sector at all? The Federal Reserve can readily provide all of the liquidity a Federal Infrastructure Bank requires to fund every worthwhile project. We can quickly move from the drawing board to construction. The books will balance. Just as the Federal Reserve recently employed Quantitative Easing to indirectly inject trillions of dollars into the economy, the Federal Reserve can just as easily capitalize a Federal Infrastructure Bank from the same toolbox.

As mentioned earlier, Quantitative Easing was believed at the time to be a desperate measure that risked triggering runaway inflation and other international monetary calamities. Of course that did not happen. Instead the American and World economy accepted a multi-trillion dollar shot of digital dollars into the United States economy with hardly a ripple. Contrary to the dire predictions, inflation remained low and the U.S. dollar gained substantially against foreign currencies, 50% against the Yen, for example.

Close observers of all of this can and will debate whether the Federal Reserve was just lucky. The Hail Mary pass was completed in the end zone. But serendipity, the accidental occurrence of positive unexpected consequences, is a powerful force in science, even the dismal science of economics. Whether it is the discovery of penicillin or an expanding universe, discoveries are made in unexpected ways. Quantitative Easing proved that monetary policy can be used to advance the economy without the dangers previously predicted.

Which means we do not need to tax our way to funding infrastructure nor do we need to pull existing money out of the commercial lending market with the consequential increase in interest rates and smothering of young companies. Further, having solved the funding challenge, hundreds of billions of dollars can quickly flow into the economy, creating millions of high paying jobs across the Nation while also reinforcing American competitiveness. There will also be something solid and permanent to show for it – this makes it politically viable.

Better still, this is money that flows into the Middle Class and that can begin to restore the purchasing power and personal savings that have been lost over the past forty years as wealth has shifted to the top 1%. To be sure, some of the new money will trickle up to the 1%, but only after it has circulated through the economy with a powerful multiplying effect.

Every rational congressman agrees that investing in infrastructure is a key to rebuilding the Middle Class. Dr. Kanter has shown us what to do with that money, so let's do it.

"The vast majority of Americans, at all Coordinates of the economic spectrum, Consider themselves middle class; this is a Deeply ingrained, distinctly American Cognitive dissonance."

Ellen Cushing

****

QUESTION:

How Can We Rebuild the Middle Class?

Answer: Through a combination of policy and monetary changes that can restore opportunities and allow working people to recover from the recession and rebuild wealth for themselves and their families.

****

A Better Congress Will (for starters):

➢ Establish an Infrastructure Bank as previously discussed to stimulate hiring, manufacturing, and to strengthen our economy.

➢ Increase the minimum wage to a living wage indexed to inflation.

➢ Establish an Education Bank to finance 100% of the costs of vocational training or higher education and as a means through which all existing education debt may be refinanced at low interest.

➢ Establish a Federal Small Business Bank to redirect Federal Reserve assets to small business underserved by private banks.

➤ Finish the work begun with the Affordable Care Act to assure health care access for all, and eliminating co-pays and deductibles.

➤ Establish a program to assist families supporting persons 75 years of age and older, and also those not yet 75 afflicted with disabling diseases of the mind and body.

➤ Require strict enforcement of trade agreements that require that those seeking to export their goods to the United States meet the negotiated standard for fair working conditions and environmental protection.

****

Discussion:

As this book is being written there are many who are celebrating an end to the Great Recession of 2008. Certainly many of the usual statistical measures give this impression. Unemployment is at levels below the pre-recession mark. The stock market indices are at historic highs. And yet, this recovery has not reached the vast majority of Americans, many of whom lost everything. For those who hung on the road back has been steep.

Housing starts are less than half the Pre-Recession levels. Wages remain stagnant with minimal gain in the average family income over the past forty years. At the same time job security and benefits that were taken for granted by earlier generations are being lost or devalued.

Those who lost their homes, and the equity they represented, are barely beginning the process of recovery seven years later. If they are employed at all they are essentially starting again from scratch, without savings, and with cost of retirement approaching. Meanwhile budget hawks constantly demand a reduction in the very social safety nets that are needed now more than ever.

It is also a cruel irony that the blessings of a longer life are mixed with the economic burden of supporting our elders. Retirement nest eggs are rarely sufficient to carry an older couple through the infirmities of old age, and particularly the cost of home care and around the clock support that is not included by Medicare. Those states offering long term care as a Medicaid benefit typically require that the elder essentially exhaust all assets and savings to be eligible for an often inadequate subsidy.

Students who have borrowed heavily to finance their education often suffer the disappointment of no jobs demanding those skills, and the weight of that debt holds them back.

Others, unwilling to incur the debt, do not even try. Add to that the heartbreaking frequency of cases where parents and grandparents have co-signed student loans and now find themselves trapped in poverty.

Outlined above in the "A Better Congress Will" section are a handful of measures that can make a powerful and nearly immediate difference. The goal is to simultaneously relieve the existing burdens on the Middle Class while at the same time creating an opportunity to rebuild family wealth and security.

"No business which depends for existence on paying less than living wages to its workers has any right to continue in this country. By living wages I mean more than a bare subsistence level --I mean the wages of decent living."

Franklin D. Roosevelt

"Today in America, unions have a secure place in our industrial life. Only a handful of reactionaries harbor the ugly thought of breaking unions and depriving working men and women of the right to join the union of their choice. I have no use for those -- regardless of their political party -- who hold some vain and foolish dream of spinning the clock back to days when organized labor was huddled, almost as a hapless mass."

Dwight D. Eisenhower

****

QUESTION:

Do You Support Collective Bargaining?

Answer: Yes. A balance of negotiating strength between labor and management is essential to assuring fair compensation and stability.

****

A Better Congress Will:

> ➢ Review labor laws to repair any provisions that do not serve the goal of creating fair balance between management and labor.

> ➢ Amend the laws as needed to assure that those who benefit by being part of a collective bargaining unit also fairly share the costs associated with such membership.

> ➢ Strengthen the rights and protections of those who believe their union management is not protecting their interests to seek a speedy hearing of their grievances from neutral judges with the power to order fair and appropriate relief.

****

Discussion:

There has always been, and always will be, a natural tension between those with capital wishing to hire individuals – and those who are hired and who seek the best compensation and treatment they can negotiate in exchange for their time. When those seeking work are plentiful, which has historically been the case more often than not, the power rests with capital and workers compete with each other.

About a century ago there was an evolution away from this model as workers in key industries began to organize, withhold and pool their labor (just as the wealthy pool their money) in exchange for greater compensation and better working conditions. At about the same time progressives in government began to adopt laws establishing work rules, restricting child labor, and compensation programs for those injured on the job. Eventually national laws were passed granting workers the right to organize, and to assure safe working conditions.

With these changes America became the industrial leader of the World. Wars were fought, highways were built, and universities were established and thrived – all supported by a working and optimistic Middle Class. That same Middle Class became consumers of those products and services.

Although unions still exist they are under constant attack and those who would move us back to the pre-organized labor days have been gaining strength and exploiting their ability to promote political candidates devoted to undoing the fabric of the American economy. For example, Governor Scott Walker of Wisconsin has risen to national prominence on the strength of his union busting success.

According to the Bureau of Labor Statistics, the number of workers who belonged to a union in 2014 was 11%. This is a loss of nearly 50% since a similar study in 1983. That statistic roughly parallels the anti-labor impact of government policies started during the Reagan administration and economic globalization that have forced American labor to compete with subsistence paid workers in Mexico,

China, Korea, Malaysia, India, Pakistan, Vietnam and elsewhere.

Even as Unions in the United States were being challenged to improve productivity and accept lower wages and benefits in order to meet foreign competition, the political right engaged in a steady drumbeat of anti-union rhetoric intended to convince Americans who were not part of an organized unit that somehow union members were to blame for the collapse of our steel, textile and other industries.

As Governor Walker demonstrated better than anyone, the extreme right has succeeded in creating a tension within the working class aimed, not at increasing the level of pay and benefits for all Americans, but rather toward bringing down those who had achieved such rewards after generations of hard work and unity with their fellow employees.

This was seen most vividly in 2013 and 2014 in Wisconsin, once the heart of organized labor, where Governor Walker cynically pitted groups of government workers against each other while whipping up an anti-union fervor among taxpayers in general who were told that their tax burden was principally the fault of public employees.

Rather than making any attempt to stimulate the economy to create greater opportunity for all in

Wisconsin, Governor Walker and his allies simply sought to destroy public unions and claim it as a victory for the average working man and woman. This provoked a recall vote which the Governor won with the help of massive infusions of campaign funding from those determined to break unions everywhere.

We see the effects of this anti-union propaganda beyond Wisconsin. Calls for privatization of schools are often an indirect attack on teachers and their unions. Air traffic controllers, the union President Reagan effectively broke over thirty years ago, have recently capitulated and now favor privatization of the air traffic management system simply because the Republican/Tea Party controlled Congress refuses to appropriate the resources desperately needed to upgrade the air management system. These air traffic professionals, upon whom the flying public relies for our lives, are prepared to take their chances in the private sector. Air safety awarded to the lowest bidder. That is reassuring.

To a great extent the 2015 debate about the Trans-Pacific Partnership (TPP) trade treaty is about unions. Many see the North American Free Trade Agreement (NAFTA), as having been the trigger for massive relocation of manufacturing jobs from the

United States to Mexico where wages and benefits are measured in pennies on the dollar. Although President Obama campaigned against NAFTA in 2008, he now repeatedly assures us that the TPP will be different. Many Americans do not believe it. Rather they see this deal as closing the door on our last chance to demand true and fair trade parity in the Pacific.

Although the TPP has been granted fast track authority there remains an eventual Congressional vote on the Treaty itself. Unless, as promised, the deal is substantially better than NAFTA, it is unlikely the American People will support any member of Congress who votes in favor.

There is a point at which the free trade advocate becomes a chump.

A Better Congress must stand up for Americans. It is time for renewed solidarity. True patriotism means finding ways to elevate all Americans.

"The crisis and recession have led to very Low interest rates, it is true, but these Events have also destroyed jobs, hamstrung Economic growth and led to sharp declines In the values of many homes and Businesses."

Ben Bernanke

"Too big to fail is too big to exist."

Bernie Sanders

****

QUESTION:

Is There Too Much Bank Deregulation?

Answer: Financial institutions are naturally inclined to expansion and maximum leveraging of assets without regard to the potential international adverse consequences of their conduct. Such institutions should not be allowed to grow to the point where their failure imperils the greater economy. Also, infusions of liquidity into the economy by the Federal Reserve is best done in a more distributive way through community investments and with a trickle up, rather than trickle down, strategy.

****

A Better Congress Will:

> ➤ Restore the restrictions on banks that limited their ability to use depositor funds for speculative investments.

➢ Amend the anti-trust laws to establish a formula for determining the maximum safe size for banks and similar financial institutions.

➢ Develop guidelines for the Federal Reserve directing that infusions of liquidity be biased in favor of distributed, rather than centralized, financial institutions.

****

Discussion:

During the early crisis days of the 2008 collapse, then Secretary of the Treasury Hank Paulson, a former chairman of one of the largest of the Wall Street investment banks, announced a massive bail-out program for the huge institutions that had created the crisis. Once the particulars were announced, a reporter asked if the United States would require the highly paid executives of these investment houses and banks to restrict their compensation until the American people had been repaid.

What was seen on Mr. Paulson's face at that moment was a look of shock at the suggestion. He mumbled something about how that would not be right, and he shortly left the podium. Right there, in that unguarded moment, the truth of what was happening could be seen.

Even with the financial architecture of the World about to collapse, Secretary Paulson could not quite get it. The men and women running these massive companies had conducted themselves irresponsibly, imperiling not just their own firms, but the World economy, yet somehow Mr. Paulson could not seem to connect the dots between their special and protected status and the damage they had done.

In his World, which was the World of Wall Street and the largest of the large corporations, his peers were to be protected. The rest of the Country could go to Hell, but Wall Street bankers should be able to keep their fantastic salaries and bonuses – paid for with American bail outs.

Through the next several years, as the baton of Treasury Secretary was handed off by Mr. Paulson, to Timothy Geithner, this pattern continued. There were massive infusions of capital into Wall Street banks, purchases of toxic assets that were unwanted by the private sector, acquisition of equity positions in AIG and other corporations – all without serious consequence to the insiders who had caused the crisis in the first instance.

There were a few shaking their fists and shouting about the inequity of this. Occupy Wall Street came and went only highlighting the helplessness of those seeking some level of evenhandedness. Only the most anemic of proposals were offered to help small business and defaulting homeowners, while trillions of dollars were expended to buck up Wall Street and similarly favored institutions in Europe that had also placed risky bets on a massive scale and looked to the United States to bail them out.

As Mr. Geithner attempts to explain in his book, *Stress Test*, he believed the best he could do was a sort of triage on a global monetary scale. "Foam the runway" for the big banks. Save those he could save and, here is the rub, those *worth* saving. And to the Wall Street executives doing temporary duty in Washington this meant saving the big banks. And that, ironically, meant making them even bigger.

Those watching closely, such as now Senator Elizabeth Warren, are loudly and rightly calling for all of us to reverse this trend and to get about the business of dismantling financial institutions that by their very size render them "too big to fail"; that is to say, they hold us all hostage to their irresponsible behavior.

But she is a voice in the wilderness. There are those serving in Congress working quietly to undo all of the regulatory reforms adopted in the wake of the financial crisis of 2008. For example, some friends of the financial industry seek to loosen the regulations on small community banks such that they can also elbow their way to the same high stakes gaming tables as their Wall Street brethren. Money flows freely into the campaign chests of congressmen voting on these measures and the reliance on financial sector contributions is nothing short of addictive and corrupting.

Ever so briefly the dangers of too big to fail came home to roost. But the lessons learned have faded as those banks have become even bigger thanks to their friends.

We need a Better Congress.

*"Peace, commerce, and honest friendship
With all nations, entangling alliances
With none."*

Thomas Jefferson

****

QUESTION:

*International Trade Treaties –
Essential or Oversold?*

Answer: Free trade can help developing countries become less dependent upon subsidies from countries with less than pure motives. It can also expand markets by reducing inefficient tariffs and restrictions. That said, they rarely live up to their promise and have wrecked much of the American industrial base.

****

A Better Congress Will:

> ➢ Decline to ratify or otherwise support trade agreements without sufficient safeguards to assure that labor practices and environmental protections match our own. A level playing field for trade must be level in fact.

> ➢ Examine all existing trade treaties to determine if all sides are living up to the letter as well as the spirit of the agreements.

****

Discussion:

During the battle over the North American Free Trade Act (NAFTA), Vice President Gore famously debated Ross Perot. Mr. Perot was a brilliant, feisty, and outspoken businessman who said that NAFTA would be devastating to the American economy as he famously predicted there would be a great sucking sound as our jobs were sent to Mexico.

In essence NAFTA converted three competing trade economies into one with Canada, the United States, and Mexico eliminating tariffs and import restrictions to expand trade. Yet, by 2008, then candidate Obama was campaigning on the need to revisit the deal to enforce the labor and environmental protections that the Pact demanded.

In 2015 it is the Trans-Pacific Partnership (TPP) that is being negotiated between most of the nations of the Pacific Rim except the Philippines and (maybe) China. In an unusual alliance the President and the Congressional leadership won fast track authority whereby Congress agreed in advance to either approve or disapprove the TPP as negotiated by the administration without trying to amend it.

By now it should be clear to every American that free trade has never equaled fair trade. The great American market is opened to the World so other nations can sell to us the goods that we once manufactured for ourselves. Yes we can export more agricultural products – but is that what an industrialized nation aspires to? Since 1992, the aggregate trade deficit is $18 Trillion. Is the answer more of the same?

It is worth noting, however, that not integrating growing countries into an economic alliance with the United States runs the risk of inviting others to step in. A ready example can be seen in the Island nation of Dominica in the Caribbean. There, the Chinese have entered into secret agreements with sweeteners including a new sports stadium, highways, apartment buildings, and solar street lights. All gifts from the people of China to the people of Dominica in return for ... what? Votes in the United Nations? Military bases? It is secret, yet it is an example that economic engagement with less developed countries is sometimes preferable to forcing them into the arms of another.

In theory, at least, countries that trade with each other have an incentive not to allow political issues or nationalism to get in the way of a good deal. But it is a theory that only works if the dominant partner, here the United States, is willing to purchase that peace by sacrificing the American worker on the altar of free trade. Those of us in Western Pennsylvania have never bought the argument that unions killed the steel industry. Rather, opening the Country to foreign steel at discounted prices killed the steel industry here. And we, like the people in other parts of the Country similarly impacted by promised free trade, have long memories.

Advancing a free trade agenda on the promise that this time will be different is asking more of the American people than they can bear after decades of defending the World and sacrificing our own economy to help others. "Trust us" is borderline insulting. We elect men and women to Congress to make difficult choices, not to avoid them.

Congress must admit that as international business thrives across borders national loyalties have substantially faded. Apple, a Silicon Valley icon, is famous for its products which could easily be assembled in the United States, but are not.

Enough is enough. This is not 1946.

ARTICLE TWO

NATIONAL DEFENSE

The Questions:

How Do You Define A Vital National Interest?

Is Energy Independence a Matter
Of National Security?

How Vulnerable is the United States
To Cyber Attack?

Are You Ready to Vote to Declare War on Russia
To Defend Estonia?

Should We Restore the Draft?

What Have We Learned From Iraq
And Afghanistan?

Do You Agree that Wounded Veterans Should Go
To the Front of the Line for Treatment?

"War may be sometimes a necessary evil, but
No matter how necessary, it is always
An Evil, never a good. We will not learn how
To live together in peace by killing
Each other's children"

Jimmy Carter

****

QUESTION:

How Do You Define A Vital National Interest?

Answer: A matter of economic or military concern the threatening of which will potentially have grave consequences for the people of the United States or our allies.

****

A Better Congress Will:

Take care to provide our armed forces, intelligence gathering, and diplomatic men and women all of the tools required to assure that no foe is tempted to threaten our vital national interests, and if such deterrence is insufficient then we must at all times be assured we have a complete and reliable understanding of the facts and the means to accomplish what must be done.

****

Discussion:

In his book, *Before the First Shots are Fired,* retired General Tony Zinni offers nonpartisan criticism of those too quick to commit American troops to ill-defined missions, with insufficient resources, and an incomplete understanding of the enemy motives, disposition and capabilities. Less plainly stated, but implicit in these concerns, is the unhappy tendency of presidents, enabled by a timid Congress, to deploy forces simply to do something, or at least to appear to be doing something.

Not since June 5, 1942, has the Congress of the United States actually voted to declare war. On that date we added Bulgaria, Hungary and Romania to Germany and Italy against whom War had already been declared in Europe.

Despite the failure of Congress to actually declare war since 1942, as contemplated by the Constitution, massive American armies have been deployed across the globe and routinely put in harm's way. Tens of thousands of Americans have died or suffered grievous wounds. In our name they have killed many more, including civilians of all ages. All without a clear expression of Congressional will reflecting the represented convictions of the American people. Equally strange has been the refusal of Congress to pass the revenue measures required to pay for such military action despite emphatic chest pounding. War on the credit card.

If we could claim some *pax Americana* as a result of all of this war making one might try to justify it in a broad historical sweep. But can we claim such success? Korea remains divided with nuclear weapons in the hands of a plainly unbalanced regime in the North. Vietnam was ultimately a lost war with the ironic result of a potential future alliance with that Country to offset China as a common foe.

Our invasion of Iraq in 1991 was a military success preserving and protecting America's access to the oil reserves of Saudi Arabia and Kuwait. No straight faced argument was made then, nor since, that the First Gulf War was about anything other than oil. Especially then, unimpeded access to Middle East oil was a vital national interest of the United States. The war was won in spectacularly rapid fashion with Iraqi troops demonstrating little appetite for battle, something we would have done well to remember. And then, we went back, for reasons that can most sympathetically be described as, mistaken.

In Syria and Iraq the ISIS alliance has managed to accomplish the unimaginable. They control large sections of territory and are exercising the power of a sovereign. Somehow they have friends outside of the battle theater providing arms and financial support. Like a cancer their control has spread, slowed only by American air power and resupply to what is left of the Iraqi army. Ironically, we are uneasy allies with Iran in this. It may be the threat from ISIS that helped to drive Iran and the United States together on nuclear nonproliferation.

We drift from crisis to crisis. In Congress war hawks are quick to demand that every president send troops and intervene, everywhere. And yet, a simple majority of Congress cannot be mustered to articulate a cohesive scope of intervention or commit to paying the financial cost. The simple fact that Congress cannot agree on something as profound as the lethal projection of American force to far off places speaks volumes. Where a vital national interest is truly at stake it should not be difficult to find the votes for war.

It is to our credit that Americans are prepared to fight and to sacrifice when the mission is clear and the cause is just. However, having been induced to support the Second Gulf War under false pretenses a harsh lesson has been learned the hard way. Whether it is Iran. Syria, Libya, Ukraine, or Estonia, the American people are going to be a tough sell on more war. Which is as it should be.

"As long as the United States - and the World gets its oil from the Middle East, we Will be Drawn into the endless crises that Seem endemic to the region. American Energy Independence would not only liberate Us, it would also drive down the worldwide Price Of oil."

Kathleen Troia McFarland

****

QUESTION:

Is Energy Independence a Matter Of National Security?

Answer: Yes.

****

A Better Congress Will:

> ➢ Extend the existing investment tax credits and other incentives that have so positively influenced the growth of the American solar and wind energy generation industries.

> ➢ Expand such incentives to energy storage technologies through which the intermittent generation of wind and solar systems may be captured, stored and then released as and where required.

> ➢ Adopt as a National priority development of a smart and defensible national energy grid to better assure that all corners of the Country will have energy security.

➤ Repeal all laws prohibiting the export of American fossil fuels to Europe and other areas of the world threatened with curtailment by Russia or others in a position to use the withholding of energy as a geopolitical weapon.

****

Discussion:

With gasoline prices lower than they have been for a while, and with substantial new natural gas production on line, the American public can be forgiven if they believe we have achieved energy independence. We have certainly made good progress but we are far from where we need to be to immunize ourselves and our allies from the threat of oil and natural gas boycotts and strategic curtailments of supply by those for whom energy is a weapon of mass disruption.

In March 2014 the *Washington Post* reported that 22% of Western Europe's natural gas requirements are supplied from Russia. Routinely Russian leaders threaten to disrupt these energy supplies. Until recently there was little the United States could do in response to this real or perceived leverage.

Fossil fuels have flowed from Russia to the West and hard western currencies have moved into Russia. The effect of this has been a more vulnerable and less stable World. Europe has also thus provided to Russia sufficient capital reserves to shrug off the post Crimea trade sanctions.

Meanwhile we remain at the mercy of those who control the vast remaining reserves of Middle East oil. About half of all Americans were born after the 1973 OPEC oil embargo that was intended to punish the United States for its support of Israel. If you were alive at the time, and remember waiting in long lines to purchase a ration of fuel, the memory of that experience has left its mark. And the risk remains.

After the 1973 Embargo ended, the price of foreign oil increased resulting in massive transfers of wealth from industrialized countries dependent upon Middle East oil to regimes that did not share our commitment to democracy and equal rights for women. Since 1992 the United States has accumulated an aggregate $18 trillion trade deficit, much of it for oil. We put up with this with resignation and appreciation that the only thing worse than expensive fuel is no fuel at all. In 2008, oil spiked to nearly $150 per barrel. The price quickly dropped to $35, followed by an increase to $110, followed in 2015 to a collapse to $45. As this is being written the spot price of oil is about $55 per barrel, with published predictions of it rising to $80 or falling to $15 by the end of 2015. Nobody really knows.

This price instability is not a matter of classic supply and demand, but rather the manipulation of inventories by OPEC and others seeking to discourage the development of renewable energy technologies and new American fossil fuel resources. And it is working, *really* working. The boom in U.S. energy development of oil and natural gas has become a bust with thousands of drilling rigs idled and tens of thousands of energy sector employees being laid off. Lower oil prices have also convinced many in Congress that renewable energy incentives are no longer necessary so there is little sign that the renewable energy tax incentives will be continued.

As long as the United States and our key allies allow ourselves to be at the mercy of foreign oil we have voluntarily placed our collective necks on the block. But it does not have to be this way and a Better Congress will take all of the steps to establish the United States as the OPEC of energy technology and a reliable source of exported fossil fuels, including coal and coal derivatives.

Tax policy encouraging solar and wind development must be expanded to include energy storage and transmission and distribution enhancements that ultimately will shrink the need for and desirability of fossil fuels. But for now, fossil fuels and nuclear power are needed as we must continue to fight for complete energy independence and security.

$55 oil is not the new normal. It is a temporary respite, a seduction by those seeking to lure the United States into a false sense of complacency. Rather, we should be exploiting this pause as an opportunity for America and its allies to complete the process of gaining true energy independence. A continuing failure to do this will inevitably destabilize the World with potentially catastrophic consequences. The annexing of Crimea by Russia should be warning enough.

"If we are to survive the progress offered by Our technologies and enjoy their abundant Bounty, we must first develop adaptive Mechanisms of security that can match or Exceed the exponential pace of the threats Before us. There's no time to lose."

Marc Goodman

****

QUESTION:

How Vulnerable is the United States To Cyber Attack?

Answer: As the United States becomes more dependent upon computers and the Internet that connects them, the danger of catastrophic failure from a malicious attack grows daily.

****

A Better Congress Will:

> ➤ Fully fund the national security agencies devoted to developing offensive and defensive capabilities for cyber warfare.

> ➤ Require a hardening of all utility and critical control systems to insulate them from cyber intrusions.

> ➤ Fund contingency planning to assure continuity of critical services in the event of a successful national scale disruption of the Internet.

****

Discussion:

In January 2015, President Obama submitted proposals to Congress to strengthen the legislative tools available to combat cyber security threats. Of course, since it was the President's suggestion, the Republican/Tea Party controlled Congress failed to act. Then, three months later, news broke about the largest cyber attack in history (so far) with millions of Federal employee records being compromised. In June 2015 the President again challenged Congress to act. Do not hold your breath.

When we speak of cyber-attack, what exactly are we talking about? In a 2012 law review article *The Law of Cyber-Attack*, Oona Hathaway and several Yale law school colleagues discussed the definition of cyber warfare and cyber attack. Their recommended definition is "any action taken to undermine the functions of a computer network for a political or national security purpose."

Unauthorized access to private records, civilian, commercial and military, is constant. Years ago a datacenter manager pointed to a bank of servers with energetically flashing lights and explained that they existed as the fire wall between the Internet attackers and the valuable data being stored by the data center. When asked how many attacks there were per day the answer was "tens of thousands". Those were the good old days.

There was a time when the objective of a cyber intrusion was simple sport, to crash a system. One of the more common threats were DOS, Denial of Service, attacks which involved simply overwhelming a targeted network to the point that it crashed. If the targeted network was supporting a critical function, such as air traffic control, the consequences were especially serious.

With time the goals of the attackers have become more ambitious. Now the objective is data. In the books, *Big Data*, and *Data and Goliath*, the scope of information available through the Internet is discussed in alarming detail. Recent invasions of the Sony and Target Store computers have vividly demonstrated that even companies with substantial financial resources cannot stop determined hackers.

At a personal level many of us have seen our identities stolen, credit cards compromised, and medical records scrutinized. Some of this is just malicious and irksome, without seriously threatening our health or safety. But the risks are much greater now as every meaningful corporation and system is vulnerable to a committed attack.

With the recent and very public attack on Sony

we witnessed the perceived retaliation of a relatively anemic foreign government, North Korea. The provocation was a juvenile movie insulting the leader of that unstable Country and deliberately provoking a response.

Setting aside the nature and recklessness of the supposed expression of free speech, the message learned from the episode is that it does not take very much to set these things off. In a sense we are fortunate that the impact of the North Korean attack was at least well aimed. They were upset with Sony and they hit Sony. Not much collateral damage. But these events are a warning that all systems are vulnerable.

Facts are hard to come by but China is suspected as the likely source behind the massive compromise of Federal employee records. Even this most recent attack of the collected data of the United States government is but a warning. According to a report from the Government Accountability Office virtually every Federal Agency considers itself vulnerable to cyber attack.

It is just a matter of time until there is a more serious event. A coordinated and sustained cyber attack by a determined enemy could disrupt the Internet for longer than we care to think about.

Should that happen how will our economy survive?

We have become dependent upon telecommunications that are integrated into phone systems that are, in turn, connected through the Internet. It is a mistake to believe it will be roughly the equivalent of being without electricity for a few days after a weather event. This will be more than inconvenient. Prolonged loss of the Internet can bring the United States to its knees for months, or longer.

This is not a joke. Bruce Schneier, a recognized expert on cyber security, details the personal and governmental cyber risks in his blog *Schneier on Security* as well as his recent book, *Data and Goliath*. He writes thoughtfully about the limits of cyber security and the roles of the NSA and U.S. CyberCommand. Add to that the Navy's 10th Fleet Cyber Command – no ships – just computers and brilliant Patriots trying to stay one step ahead of the bad guys.

As Mr. Schneider writes,

> "[W]hat's the threat dynamic, and what's the nature of the world? The threat is going to increase; it's going to get worse, not better; cyber is a great equalizer. Cyber doesn't recognize physical geography."

Now is not the time for finger pointing, Monday morning quarterbacking, or ignoring this increased threat. The Republican/Tea Party coalition is going to have to share the work and the credit with the Administration. The consequences of inaction are too extreme

A Better Congress will act and support real legislative efforts aimed at anticipating and meeting this unprecedented threat.

"Never, never, never believe any war will be
Smooth and easy, or that anyone who
Embarks on the strange voyage can measure
The tides and hurricanes he will encounter.
The statesman who yields to war fever must
Realize that once the signal is given, he is
No longer the master of policy but the slave
Of unforeseeable and uncontrollable events."

Sir Winston Churchill

****

QUESTION:

Are You Ready to Vote to Declare War on Russia to Defend Estonia?

Answer: If we are serious about our alliances, yes.

****

A Better Congress Will:

> ➢ Take care to engage in alliances only in situations and with Countries where we sincerely are prepared to go to war in their defense.

> ➢ Pass all necessary appropriations to assure our armed forces have everything they require to deter an attack on an ally.

> ➢ Require of our allies behavior and responsible conduct that will not unreasonably provoke an attack by Russia or any other dangerous international actor.

****

Discussion:

Article 5 of the North Atlantic Treaty, the basis for the North Atlantic Treaty Organization (NATO), pledges each member to come to the aid of any other member that is attacked by a force outside of the alliance. Originally designed to organize the collective defense of the Western European and North American powers during the height of the Cold War, NATO could have gone one of two ways with the fall of the Soviet Union.

It could have declared victory and dissolved. Or, as it ultimately did, it could quickly embrace the weak Baltic States, formerly of the USSR, and cast the NATO umbrella over those countries that have for centuries been conquered, reconquered, and ultimately controlled by Russia. During the relatively brief time between the collapse of the USSR and the exploitation of Russian fossil fuel resulting in a reenergized Russia, the NATO members gambled that they could militarily integrate Estonia, Lithuania, and Latvia into NATO, and their former spouse would not mind. That was wishful thinking.

Embittered former Soviets like Vladimir Putin are feeling their petrodollar oats and are pushing the World toward another war. The weaker sisters are being picked off first. Goodbye Crimea, and the rest of Ukraine is hanging by a thread.

In Ukraine we see a nation that unsuccessfully tried to engage the West while not unduly upsetting its Russian neighbor, its indispensible source of natural gas. For a while Russia played by our rules. It essentially tried to purchase the loyalty of Ukraine by negotiating an advantageous trade and subsidy package.

Much to the chagrin of Russian leaders a revolution in Ukraine replaced their friends with those more inclined to trade with the West. The new government reneged on its deal with Russia and, predictably, the Russian leadership decided to go back to old school rules of diplomacy. In short order the Crimea was part of Russia with little serious fuss by the West.

Western trade sanctions have been painful to the average Russian, but survivable. Worse, and as is often the case, the suffering caused by the trade sanctions has only hardened the resolve of the people who share a patriotic pride over the bit by bit reassembly of the USSR. Even more to the point, and in an echo of the years leading to World War II, Russia learned that the West, including the United States, could be tested. Crimea was expendable, just as Czechoslovakia had been in 1938. So, how about war over Estonia?

It is more than possible that Russia will threaten Estonia, Latvia and Lithuania. It may even be probable. The excuse will be that there are many ethnic Russians in those Countries who believe themselves to be oppressed, just as many in Crimea claimed to be. And what will we do about it? If we follow our NATO Treaty obligation we must go to the aid of our ally.

Are we seriously prepared to do so? If yes, we need to be much clearer about that than we have been. During the summer of 2015 there have been statements that NATO will be stationing troops and tanks in the Baltic Member Countries. Russia has already announced it will reciprocate with more troops stationed on its borders with those Countries. And so it begins.

If we are not serious about defending Estonia, and the others, then we need to decide for how long we can carry the bluff. We have some practice in this.

Taiwan has been under the threat of attack from the People's Republic of China for generations. It is practically a cliché that every new United States president will be tested with some bellicose threat from the PRC against Taiwan requiring a deployment of a U.S. carrier group. For years the threats have been hollow. But with the growth of the PRC Navy, especially in submarines, and the weakening of our own forces, the time may come when we have to decide whether we are prepared to risk it all over Taiwan.

Dangerous errors occur when line in the sand declarations are made without the ability or intent to follow through. Threats to use the might of the American military must be credible. During the 1973 Yom Kippur War between Israel and Egypt, President Nixon had to do much more than rattle the saber to persuade the USSR to lean on its then allies to back away. We had to threaten war, and mean it. In this the Soviets were also aware that President Nixon was dealing with a domestic political crisis and might therefore act unreasonably as a matter of internal politics. The silver lining to Watergate.

Most recently President Obama, reported to be an excellent poker player, found out in Syria what happens when your bluff is called. He declared chemical weapons use by the Syrian government would be the red line that if crossed would provoke substantial American intervention. Chemical weapons were used. Ultimately, and to our collective chagrin, we had to rely on Russia to help us save face through the negotiation of a Syrian chemical weapons reduction program, a program that has never been completed, if ever seriously started.

Egg remains on the President's face and he has been substantially weakened. Sorry to say.

So, would any particular congressman vote to go to war over Estonia? The public answer must be "yes". They are our NATO ally, and any statement short of absolute support all but invites Russia to reclaim what it believes has always been hers. But would we, really?

"The Iraq war was fought by one-half of one Percent of us. And unless we were part of That small group or had a relative who was, We went about our lives as usual most of the Time: no draft, no new taxes, no changes. Not so for the small group who fought the War and their families."

Bob Schieffer

****

QUESTION:

Should We Restore the Draft?

Answer: No.

****

A Better Congress Will:

Restore and maintain the selective service infrastructure and keep in place the procedures to enable a restoration of the draft quickly if required.

****

Discussion:

Armies raised are armies used.

Having essentially demobilized after World War I, the United States allowed its army and tiny air force to whither to the point where our land forces under arms ranked below many smaller countries.

Our navy was formidable, although aging. As it became likely we would be dragged into another war in Europe the United States resumed the draft by the narrowest of votes in the House of Representatives on August 12, 1941. Just four months before the attack on Pearl Harbor.

According to the National World War II Museum, the combined armed forces of the United States grew from 334,473 in 1939 to 12,209,238 by 1945. Of these over 61% were drafted. This last statistic may be a surprise to those who prefer to believe that Americans overwhelmingly volunteered to serve. Many did, but most did not. And that was a far less ambiguous war then those to which we have become accustomed ever since.

Reviewing additional data from the same source, during the Second World War 38.8% of the American armed forces served in non-combat rear echelon roles. The probability of injury or death from combat was 22 in 1000. Point being that even in what was ultimately accepted to be a just war, with a remote probability of death or combat wounds, most of the service personnel were draftees.

Moving forward to Vietnam, and according to the National Vietnam Veterans Association, 25% of those deployed to Vietnam were draftees and they represented over 30% of those killed in action. Draft deferments for going to college and otherwise were considered by many to be unfair. There was also a perception that draftees were more likely to be assigned combat roles. Resentment against the draft was a significant reason the public did not support the war and ultimately President Johnson was driven from office by the antiwar factions of his own Party.

President Nixon cancelled the draft calls scheduled for the end of 1969 and ultimately the United States transitioned to an all-volunteer force. Since then, from time to time the question is raised: should we reinstate the draft? The short answer is really a single word question: why? Given the high tech nature of modern warfare and the importance of expensive and repetitive training, what is the advantage to involuntarily cycling millions of young people through a military training that will ill equip them for the wars we have been fighting?

Many say it will help solidify the national spirit of Americans to have a common experience of service, which of course suggests there is no national spirit or sense of shared purpose and sacrifice already. Is that true?

Others note that the volunteer armed forces are especially attractive to the poor for whom there are fewer competing options for upward mobility. The effect of this, it is argued, is that we send our less financially advantaged to fight our wars for us while the better off stay home. Extending this argument some say that a draft affecting all economic classes would make war less likely as the rich would be dying with the poor.

A third group argues that even a generalized minimal experience with basic military discipline and training will better prepare the nation for mobilization should the time (when the time?) comes that we must defend our Country from a determined and well armed foe.

Taking all of the above into consideration there is in opposition to these arguments the simple truth that armies raised are armies used. Having an expensive force readily at hand, perpetually mobilized as it has been since the end of World War II, is a temptation for those who equate might with right. We have sufficient forces to deal with the actual threats that face us. In addition, with the evolution of robotic warfare the need for slightly trained personnel to make mass attacks has lessened or become utterly obsolete.

That said, the time may come when a draft is necessary. And therefore Congress should maintain the ability to quickly and efficiently reinstate conscription. It will do no harm for every young person to know they may be called upon to serve. They may even consider taking an interest in current events.

"I can't tell you if the use of force in Iraq Today will last five days, five weeks or five Months, but it won't last any longer than That."

Donald Rumsfeld

****

QUESTION:

What Have We Learned From Iraq And Afghanistan?

Answer: The limitations of American power, again.

****

A Better Congress Will:

> ➤ Demand of the administration compelling arguments and proof of grounds justifying the commitment of American forces.

> ➤ Finance any wars or military interventions it authorizes with appropriate tax increases.

> ➤ Avoid irresponsible and bellicose statements intended to inflame the American people unless those same elected officials are prepared to put their political careers on the line and vote for war and the revenues to pay for it.

****

Discussion:

America was watching when on February 5, 2003, while fighting a miserable cold, then Secretary of State Colin Powell spoke to the United Nations to present the proof that made his government absolutely certain that Saddam Hussein's Iraq was manufacturing, and intending to use, weapons of mass destruction. One of the most trusted men in America was putting it all on the line. Ten years later he admitted he was wrong. But by then we were deeply involved in what has been the longest continuous war in American history. Based on a mistake, or worse.

Secretary Powell was not alone in this. His eventual successor, Hillary Clinton, has been trying to explain her Senate vote for the war for over a decade. In both cases their defense is they were lied to by people they trusted and counted on to find the facts and report them accurately and completely to those making the decisions. How such a catastrophic error could be made has been the topic of many books since. Someone else is always to blame.

It is reminiscent of an episode in 1999 during our air war in Yugoslavia under President Bill Clinton. On May 7th, the United States dropped precision ordinance on a target in Belgrade that was identified by the Central Intelligence Agency as the Yugoslav Federal Directorate for Supply and Procurement. In fact, it was the Embassy of the People's Republic of China. As later explained by CIA Director George Tenet, this was a rare target selected by the CIA and it provided the wrong coordinates to the Air Force. The real target was about 100 yards away.

Director Tenet was still in charge four years later when the CIA gave the green light to Secretary Powell to give his UN speech regarding our absolute certainty that Iraq was equipping itself with weapons of mass destruction. He even sat behind Secretary Powell at the United Nations as the Secretary of State told the World why the United States had no choice but to invade Iraq, again.

In both cases the lesson is the importance of simple humility. Director Tenet has his own side of the story, and of course it is the same as everyone else's: he was given bad intelligence.

Somewhat less controversial was our invasion of Afghanistan after September 11th. Controlled by the Taliban, that Country was used by Al-Qaeda as a safe haven and training base. There appears to be no serious factual dispute (setting aside the persistent conspiracy theories to the contrary) that the

September 11th attacks were planned and directed from Afghanistan, under the direction of Al-Qaeda, and specifically planned by the group lead by Osama bin Laden. Given an opportunity to surrender bin Laden, or to at least cooperate with our efforts, the Taliban refused and left America and her allies no choice. The Taliban forces and leadership, along with many innocent civilians, would suffer the consequences of the Taliban's complicity before, during, and after the September 11th attacks. So the cause was just. But the execution?

A few months before September 11th this writer was attending the graduation of his stepson from the Naval Academy at Annapolis, Maryland. It was a beautiful day, although low cloud cover prevented the traditional fly over by the Flying Angels. The speaker was the new President, George W. Bush, who had been on the job about four months.

During the course of his remarks the President thanked the new ensigns before him, for their commitment to service. Interestingly though, he went on to tell them that they would only be required briefly as the military would be down-sizing. The World situation was such that the United States no longer required masses of troops and ships. Those thinking about a career in the Navy, he said, should consider other options. So much for being an inspirational leader.

This story is worth telling as it revealed the temperament of the new Administration and particularly the once again Secretary of Defense, Donald Rumsfeld, who had served in the same post 25 years before. Secretary Rumsfeld was pressing for a smaller military to reduce the cost of government. That this was the plan had been previously revealed and it reflected a terrible miscalculation that the wars of the future could be tidy affairs fought with a minimum of troops employing sophisticated weapons and precision ordinance.

As a result, the eventual deployment to Afghanistan after September 11th was inadequate and bin Laden escaped to Pakistan. In their frustration the President and his team elected to expand the American military footprint to Iraq. When General Eric K. Shinseki testified before Congress that an invasion of Iraq would require several hundred thousand troops, Secretary Rumsfeld sent his Deputy, Paul D. Wolfowitz, to the Capitol to contradict the General, calling his estimate "wildly off the mark". Closer to 100,000 troops would be required, according to Mr. Wolfowitz. In other words the President and his Secretary of Defense were planning a war on best case assumptions and with a predisposition to believe that this war, and all future wars, could be fought and won on the cheap and by remote control.

Fortunately President Obama, who openly opposed the second Iraq War from the start, has honored his campaign promise to mostly extract the United States from Iraq and Afghanistan. He has also resisted the temptation to commit American troops to Libya, Syria and Ukraine despite calls from war hawks in Congress and cable news talking heads to do so. No question the Obama Administration has lurched from time to time and stumbled. But we no longer have masses of troops deployed where America's vital National interests are not at stake. Our reputation is bruised, but most of our sons and daughters are home.

Given the realities of budget cuts and the cost of modern systems, the United States simply cannot afford wars to preserve its national ego and extend the past glories of World War II. To his credit, President Obama has displayed a healthy skepticism for the reliability of intelligence. He rightly wants to be sure of what he is doing and why he is doing it.

And so, at least for now, important lessons have been learned.

"Damn the wars but bless the soldier."

T.L. Moffitt

****

QUESTION:

Do You Agree that Wounded Veterans Should Go To the Front of the Line for Treatment?

Answer: Yes.

****

A Better Congress Will:

> ➤ Fully Fund Veterans Affairs to assure that veterans in need of services are served without unreasonable delay.

> ➤ Authorize veterans to seek care outside of the VA and at government expense in the event a veteran believes their needs can be better met through the private sector.

> ➤ Establish a fully staffed and trained intervention office that any veteran can call upon to resolve red tape issues and bottlenecks. Each such call should generate not only immediate resolution, but also an inquiry as to why such intervention was required, all to identify and correct procedures that are failing to meet the needs of veterans.

➢ Provide Veterans with symptoms of PTSD and similar injuries immediate and effective treatment and support.

****

Discussion:

At the Veterans Affairs government website, one can find an impressive array of reports, plans, and strategies – pretty much everything but an apology.

However, we are told that the VA has 152 hospitals, 800 community-based outpatient clinics, 161 nursing homes, and 147 national cemeteries representing the final resting place of over 3.7 Million Americans. We are also advised that 22 Million veterans are still living and entitled to the honors they deserve from a grateful Nation.

This writer never served in the Military. Most have not served. Three of the last five Presidents were elected without any military experience and one of the two who did serve was never deployed overseas. All of that makes the debt ever the more acute and the need to do right by those that have served that much more important as a matter of National honor.

As noted above the VA is huge. By and large it executes its mission well albeit with a maddening lack of efficiency that can often be explained by the refusal of Congress to provide the up to date computers and software required. This failure to fully fund the needs of the VA is as shocking and inexcusable as the sending of troops to Iraq without sufficiently armored vehicles. Contrary to the glib remarks of one Secretary of Defense that "you go to war with the army you have, not the army you might want or wish to have" – in fact we go to war - and we care for its wounded with the resources we choose to provide.

Since the sordid facts of fraud and secret waiting lists came to light some Members of Congress have repeatedly taken cheap shots at the Agency with demands for discipline and withholding of compensation until and unless it fully performs the tasks for which its employees are paid. By that standard no Congressman should have received a pay check since the balanced budget days of the Clinton Administration. Hypocrisy is unbecoming, especially from legislators who have failed to live up to their responsibilities to assure that the VA has all of the tools and personnel required and to conduct effective oversight.

Conservatives are champions of choice (usually) and as champions of choice we can expect the Republican/Tea Party coalition controlling Congress to take immediate and unequivocal steps to authorize Veterans to reject the VA and seek better care in the private sector. Health care providers should also be guided by legislation that offers a meaningful bonus payment if Veterans are seen within three business days of making their appointments. Yes, Veterans should go to the front of the line. They have earned it.

ARTICLE THREE

HEALTH CARE AND ELDER CARE

The Questions:

How Can We Support 40 Million Americans Over 75 Years Old?

Can Social Security or Medicare Ever Go Broke?

Do You Agree that Inequality of Health Care Is Unjust?

What Is The "Value Added" From Private Insurance Companies?

What is the Connection Between Spirituality And Health Care Reform?

Do You Support Replacing Medical Malpractice Litigation With A Better Compensation System?

Should We Get Serious About a Curriculum Of Wellness in Our Schools?

"Caring for others tends to be the first cut
When we review our personal time budget. It
Does not necessarily fulfill the goals of my
Ambition; it will not pave the way for my
Success; it takes away from my own
Depleted emotional resources. It is an
Imposition in every way. To some of us, it is
An inconvenience from which we
Unashamedly run. We have become experts
In maintaining a grand scope of friendships
And amateurs in genuine intimacy and care.
Unwittingly, we have sacrificed everything
On the altar of self-sufficiency—only to
Discover that we have sold our souls to
Isolation."

Sandy Yoshiro Rosen

****

QUESTION:

How Can We Support 40 Million Americans Over 75 Years Old?

Answer: Through a combination of technology, volunteerism, and acceptance of the financial cost as a shared national obligation.

****

A Better Congress Will:

> ➢ Pass legislation providing financial support for those aged 75, or younger if they have acquired severe memory impairment or disabilities.

- ➢ Recognize a refundable tax credit for home based services and technology for the elderly.

- ➢ Qualify family and friends who take elders into their homes for subsidies to help offset the added costs.

- ➢ Eliminate Medicare caps on rehabilitative care.

****

Discussion:

Based upon the most recent U.S. Census Bureau figures, as of 2012 there were 18 Million Americans 75 years old and older. The total over 65 but not yet 75 was 23 Million. So in ten years we can estimate there will be about 40 Million Americans over the age of 75. Of this number, absent a medical breakthrough, at least half will eventually suffer from Alzheimer's disease or equally devastating other memory loss and physical disabilities. Surviving to age 100 is no longer a newsworthy achievement, but there is no avoiding the frailties that come with that milestone.

At the same time, the demographic profile of the United States will show a reduction in Americans still in their productive years. By 2025, the number of people 18 years to 70 years, and able to work productively will be inadequate to support the general economy while at the same time providing support and health care services to our elders.

Economists refer to this as the "Dependency Ratio" and most often it comes up in the discussion of the long term financial viability of Social Security and Medicare. With so much money needed to pay for the care for the over 75 population the existing tax schemes are insufficient.

Even those retirees fortunate enough to have accumulated a nest egg and with plans to live frugally on their Social Security, quickly find that the existing social safety net is filled with holes. Savings can be swiftly consumed with uncovered medical costs. Custodial care is not covered at all. Children and grandchildren with their own financial challenges are often called upon to subsidize the care of their elders. Ultimately, and sooner than expected, a lifetime of savings is exhausted and younger family members are expected to sacrifice their own savings to support their parents and grandparents.

Maddeningly the standard Republican/Tea Party response is to ignore the problem. Simply not discuss it. For to discuss it is to reveal this awkward truth: we cannot cut, save or tax our way out of this crisis. Cutting government safety programs just shifts the problem to the elderly and their families. It may reduce taxes, which is what the Insatiable Wealthy crave, but it does not solve the problem – it simply moves if off the Federal budget.

Many head in the sand conservatives in Congress also insist that we all should become more frugal and save for our retirements and future disabilities. Take some personal responsibility they insist, as they calculate the value of their taxpayer funded pensions.

How exactly is that supposed to work? An average working class couple is already expected to support up to five generations: themselves, their children, perhaps their grandchildren, their parents and often their grandparents. All of this on wages that have not increased at all in forty years. How much can they be expected to save from what little remains? As the television character Archie Bunker once explained, "All of my money is tied up in staying alive." However, we can find the money. More on that shortly.

By far the most difficult challenge in meeting the needs of the elderly is finding the caretakers. It is this human resource that will be in short supply. While the number of people requiring ever increasing levels of care balloons the population available to provide those services is shrinking. This is hardly news to anyone who has attempted to hire a caretaker or companion for their elder in need.

It is not unreasonable to estimate that in the year 2025 we will need the equivalent of one full time caretaker for every person over 75 years old. To be sure, many in the elder group will not be nearly so needy – but others will require 24 hour a day care and thus their needs will consume the full time and year round attention of several adults. Of course, those caring for the infirm are not available to work in industry or other employments we consider "productive" in the sense of creating products and services for the consumer economy and export.

With a declining birth rate this is an unsustainable model. It is quite predictable that by 2025, in less than ten years from when this book is being written, the unemployment rate in the United States will be zero. Everyone capable of working will be needed and gainfully employed. And we will need more.

Allan S. "Chip" Teel, M.D., of Maine has written a useful book on a strategy combining community volunteerism, often from retirees, with technology to allow elders to stay in their own homes safely until the very end of life. *Alone and Invisible No More – How Grassroots Activism and 21st Century*

Technology Can Empower Elders to Stay in Their Own Homes and Live Healthier, Happier Lives, discusses Dr. Teel's lifetime of experience with his patients. This writer helped to edit Dr. Teel's book, and its message is especially clear.

Ask just about any elder and they will tell you that home, however they define it, is where they want to be. Home with their pets, their neighbors, family, familiar smells and most of all, the memories that are the essence of life. Elders living at home can cope very well with a surprisingly small amount of professional interaction. What is required is the technology to allow virtual house calls and 24 hour monitoring. Family, friends and local volunteers need to be part of this solution, coordinated through formal or informal networks to assure daily, or more frequent, visits and telephone calls.

To help assure the continuation of purposefulness, which is a key to happiness, the elders too can be called upon to help each other. They can and should be part of the support team for their neighbors. A scheduled call from one elder to another helps them both. By substituting the more personal touch of lay volunteers and family where ever and whenever possible the cost of care is dramatically reduced while providing for the human interaction that is essential to everyone.

As a physician who has tried all of the usual elder care management approaches, Dr. Teel has concluded that the high tech aging in place approach is the most effective and humane. It requires fewer paid staff and thus frees up workers for the traditional economy. It is also the most cost effective.

Which brings us back to money.

One way or the other we must ultimately manage the tens of millions of our elders who are financially and physically dependent. It will be expensive. Lots of money. But unlike the coolest new electronic product or car, this is not a discretionary purchase. We have no choice. We must find a way to finance the care of our elders as a matter of national and collective responsibility. Which means Congress has to step up.

This Congress? Our current Congress cannot even do the simple things – and this is not simple at all. We will need hundreds of billions of dollars over the next thirty years. If we cannot cut, save or tax our way there then what is left?

Monetary policy to the rescue, again. As discussed in response to the first question in this book, "Can the United States Bounce a Check?" the answer comes from recognition that the United States can generate as much currency as is necessary. Just as we saw with Quantitative Easing the Federal Reserve can move trillions of dollars into the economy in a targeted way without triggering runaway inflation or an international devaluing of the dollar.

In the case of our elders we can, actually we must, develop a program that funds the reasonable needs of every eligible American. If we want we can stick to the idea that retirees need to support themselves for a while. But once we reach age 75, nearly all of us will need additional financial help. What is required can flow from the Federal Reserve to a new long term care bank that in turn provides support for the reasonable choices eligible elders can make.

As this funding flows into the economy it will go directly into the pockets of the middle class workers who perform the health and custodial services, install the technology, maintain the homes, make the meals, and otherwise provide the care and support required. This same program should eliminate all of the Medicare co-pays and deductibles to assure that every elder can afford all of the medical care they need to maintain a reasonable quality of life.

As this money flows into the middle class it will also help restore part of the wages and purchasing power that has been lost by working Americans for the past forty years. For sure some of the money will trickle up to the wealthy. But along the way those dollars will circulate and recirculate among average people who are playing by the rules and working hard.

Caring for our elders is a test of national character and humanity. We can do it, but this requires a Better Congress, one prepared to roll up its sleeves, think outside the box, and get it done.

"The whole idea of "leaners" and "lifters" is
The central teaching of the right wing
Ideologue, Ayn Rand, who penned books like
The Virtue of Selfishness. It's a self-serving
Crock. Rand found out the hard way. After a
Lifetime proselytizing on behalf of the
"Producers" and denouncing anyone needing
Government assistance as "parasites," when
Rand became old and sick, she discovered
That even a bestselling author could not
Afford health care in the neoliberal US. She
Availed herself of Medicare and ended her
Life on what she had despised – social
Security."

Anne Manne

****

QUESTION:

Can Social Security or Medicare Ever Go Broke?

Answer: No.

****

A Better Congress Will:

> ➢ Reaffirm that such obligations are commitments made by the United States and that the Federal Reserve will honor all checks and payments issued to fulfill such commitments.

> Discontinue the public deception of claiming that Social Security or Medicare Trusts exist at all and plainly and candidly report to the American people that these programs are paid from current revenues.

> Amend Medicare to require competitive bidding on drugs and durable medical equipment to reduce the cost of care.

> Lift the caps on taxable income for Social Security and Medicare.

> Substantially simplify the billing and coding procedures for Medicare to reduce the cost to health care providers.

> Establish an administrative and streamlined procedure for dealing with allegations of medical negligence in cases involving Medicare. The objective will be compensation where appropriate but more importantly assurance of a rapid quality control process to identify and correct weaknesses in the delivery of care.

****

Discussion:

For those who persist in believing in Santa Claus, the Easter Bunny, the Tooth Fairy and similar pleasant fantasies, the harsh news is that the claimed Social Security Trust Fund has been bankrupt for many years. All of the excess money raised through payroll and employer taxes, supposedly to be used to fund future Social Security benefits, is instead "loaned" to the United States Treasury in exchange for a future promise to pay. Some call this the unified system. Some call it pay as you go. Whatever you call it, it should not be called a trust fund.

That said, about one trillion dollars a year in Social Security retirement, disability and survivor benefits are paid. And there will never come a time when the checks stop coming because, quite simply, Social Security can never go broke. Unless, of course, Congress decides it wants to default. As discussed in response to the very first Question answered in this book, the United States can never bounce a check, unless it wants to.

As we witnessed during the Great Recession the Federal Reserve ultimately covers every payment issued by the United States and where tax revenues and public borrowing are insufficient the difference is covered through the creation of new digital currency. A few keystrokes of a computer at the Federal Reserve and all obligations of the United States are covered.

Of course this reality can make some people nervous. These are people who actually believe money means something, as if there is a finite amount that simply moves back and forth across the economy. Of course this is not true. If it was ever true it has not been since the United States went off the gold standard in 1971.

If you feel compelled to worry about the monetary supply then it is not altogether unreasonable to ask this: is there a tipping point at which too much liquidity, too many digital dollars, entering the economy at the whim of the Federal Reserve can have adverse consequences? Yes. It is possible.

Most obvious is the worry that too many new dollars will dilute the value of the money already in circulation. This can trigger inflation, too many dollars chasing too few goods. But we have the opposite situation right now. The World is awash in goods and excess labor. There is no shortage of goods or potential workers to staff our factories.

Another theoretical concern is that other nations and international business will cease to use the dollar as the standard for international transactions. Really? When the Federal Reserve injected over two trillion dollars into the economy through its Quantitative Easing, Hail Mary pass, during the recession, the result was actually a much stronger dollar. 50% stronger compared to the Japanese Yen for example.

In fact QE worked so well that other nations have stopped fighting their recessions with austerity and have also embraced monetary easing to inject more liquidity and greater activity into their economies.

That said, and as listed above, there are a few steps Congress can take to shore up the ability of the United States to cover its Social Security promises from current tax revenues. These are more conventional and thus more likely to be adopted by those who cannot quite get their heads around the concept of digital currency.

For the purposes of this question, however, the answer is that the United States will always honor its financial obligations, including its pledge to retirees. And those who say otherwise should confess they are either clueless, or are deliberately trying to frighten the American people for political purposes.

"Of All Forms of Injustice, Inequality Of Health Care is the Most Shocking And Inhumane."

Rev. Martin Luther King, Jr.

****

QUESTION:

Do You Agree that Inequality of Health Care is Unjust?

Answer: Yes.

****

A Better Congress Will:

> ➢ Progress beyond the Affordable Care Act to assure access to quality health care for everyone in the United States.

> ➢ Eliminate co-pays and deductibles.

> ➢ Include in the National Health Care strategy mental health and substance abuse programs.

> ➢ Fund a curriculum of wellness in every school requiring in depth K through 12 age appropriate education about nutrition, exercise, first aid, caring for the elderly, all intended to elevate health education to the same rank as reading and mathematics.

****

Discussion:

There is a fairly simple test to separate the believers in health care justice from those who are more aligned with the "every man for himself" school of thought. Simply ask yourself the following question (answer honestly):

Do you believe that a homeless person in the street has the same right to quality health care as the governor of your state?

Those who answer with anything other than an unqualified "yes", are somewhere on the spectrum that equates the right to live with wealth. There can be arguments over degree and shades of gray. But, ultimately, this simple question forces all of us to look into the mirror and weigh our own humanity.

As Dr. King said, the absence of health care equality is inhumane and shocking. And yet, especially extreme conservatives are perfectly comfortable rationing health care based upon the ability to pay. Marie Antoinette would feel right at home.

How quickly many forget how it was during the years before the Affordable Care Act and Patient Protection Act were passed. Leading up to the 2008 presidential election the number of Americans who were uninsured for at least part of the year was approximately 80 Million. Of those with insurance many had "Swiss Cheese" coverage, full of holes. Or they had policies with unaffordable co-payments, deductibles, and caps that essentially rendered the person living from paycheck to paycheck virtually uninsured. For a working family a $25 co-pay for a child visit to a pediatrician, added to the costs of transportation and time from work, meant supposed health insurance was a cruel fiction.

An estimated 18,000 Americans were dying each year due to a lack of access to health care. It was the equivalent of five September 11th attacks, every year.

General Motors, which managed the largest employer sponsored health care plan in the World, was staggering toward bankruptcy even before the Great Recession. Size alone was obviously not the secret to a viable health care plan despite the frequent claims of the Bush Administration that simply allowing smaller employers to band together would somehow solve the health insurance crisis.

Before the ACA, health care costs were the number one reason for personal bankruptcy. Yet in many cases the persons who were filing actually had some sort of health insurance. It was just inadequate, or claims were routinely denied. These Americans were counted as insured, but in reality, they were effectively uninsured or only partially insured.

Nobody should die or suffer in the United States for lack of access to reasonable health care. America has it within its power to assure everyone has access to quality health care regardless of wealth or social rank. We can drive different cars and live in grand or modest homes. Some will attend Harvard while others a community college. But when it comes to our health, we all deserve quality care.

"Everyone should have health insurance? I Say everyone should have health care. I'm Not selling insurance."

Dennis Kucinich

****

QUESTION:

Is There Any Need for Private Health Insurance Companies?

Answer: Not for quality fundamental care. If there is a market for boutique health care insurance, that is fine, but there is no useful role for private insurers in the delivery of universal quality health care and they should be eliminated from the system as an unnecessary and expensive burden.

****

A Better Congress Will:

> ➢ Investigate the role of private health insurers and determine what such businesses add to the health care system that justifies the added expense and delays they cause?

> ➢ If, as expected, the conclusion of Congress is that private health insurers do not add value to the health management process that cannot be more efficiently and humanely handled through a single payer system, then a Better Congress will transition the Country to such a single payer system allowing the massive savings to be invested in assuring quality care for all.

****

Discussion:

Medicare is the single largest administrator of health care benefits in the United States. Some 55 Million Americans count on it. They are generally over 65 years of age, but younger people qualify if they are totally disabled or suffer from end stage renal disease. In other words, Medicare takes care of the sickest of us, and it does so far more cost efficiently than private insurers. Medicare is a plain example of a government run program that is more effective and more economical than its private sector counterparts.

By contrast, before passage of the Affordable Care Act and Patient Protection Act private health insurance companies were routinely consuming well in excess of 25% of premiums collected for overhead costs of administration, advertising, profits, management compensation, sales commissions, lobbying and underwriting. Medicare overhead was closer to 5%.

Meanwhile, private insurers were routinely abusing their customers through wrongful denials of claims and the simple expedient of cancelling the insurance of any customer who became chronically ill. And it was all perfectly, well maybe not perfectly, but actually legal. Consumers did not know better and were helpless to fight back. Even the so-called non-profit insurers, such as the "Blues" were over charging and under serving their customers.

Unlike private insurers, Medicare did not try to duck its responsibilities.

With the passage of the Affordable Care Act and Patient Protection Act, Congress and the President made a deal with the private health care insurance industry. Some consider it a pact with the devil, others the art of compromise.

In short, the insurance industry agreed to allow Congress to pass the reforms, without exercising its substantial political power in opposition, provided that the new system would require every American to be insured one way or the other. Mandates. Yes, those mandates. The same mandates that Republicans have tried to hang around the neck of President Obama since 2009, were actually the price of the insurance industry's cooperation. That, and private insurers demanded one more thing, no national insurance plan. No Medicare for all. The insurance industry wanted to stay in business and was not interested in competing with a more efficient player like Medicare.

So the agreement was reached and in addition to expanded health care availability the law also dramatically curtailed the most egregious of the private health insurance practices. At least 80% of collected premiums would have to actually be spent on health care. Policies could not be cancelled simply because the insured becomes ill. Young people would be allowed to stay on their parents' health insurance policies until the age of 26.

Notwithstanding the never ending howls of protest from the Republican/Tea Party coalition, who have tried no fewer than 56 times (as of this writing) to repeal the laws, the impact has been a dramatic increase in the number of Americans with health insurance of some kind. The runaway inflation in health care costs has likewise been tamed, at least for now.

Twice the Supreme Court has considered the validity of the ACA and it has survived even with a Court packed with conservative Justices.

However, in 2015, the private insurance industry is letting it be known that it plans to raise premiums dramatically. Why? Because they think they can.

Which quite naturally provokes the question, what is the purpose of private insurers and what justifies their comparatively high overhead and profits? What do the customers, the ones paying the premiums, get in return? How can we explain our willingness as a nation to pay the freight for hundreds of different health insurers each with their own administrative overhead, forms, and policies, and each doing its best to pay as little as possible for health care and whenever possible denying or delaying claims?

In fact, insurers add absolutely nothing to the health care system that could not be done equally well and more efficiently by an expansion of Medicare to all Americans. Keep in mind that Medicare already manages the needs of the elderly and the disabled. What is left are people under 65 years old who require considerably less health care.

A Better Congress will take a hard and honest look at the private health insurance industry and decide if it is really worth the added cost to Americans. The answer should be "no".

*"For in the final analysis, our most basic
Common link, is that we all inhabit this
Small planet, we all breathe the same air,
We all cherish our children's futures, and
We are all mortal."*
                              John F. Kennedy

****

QUESTION:

What is the Connection Between Spirituality and Health Care Reform?

Answer: Managing our health care choices is an intensely personal matter which becomes all the more so as we approach the end of life. This is the point at which one's acceptance of our shared mortality ultimately controls our care choices. Each of us owe it to our families and ourselves to think through our end of life plan, at what point do we exercise the ultimate liberty to decline medical interventions that only prolong, but do not enhance life. Government's role is to stay out of the way, to respect this process and avoid regulations and policies that make such choices more difficult than they already are.

****

A Better Congress Will:

> ➢ Assure that Medicare laws do not bully or pressure patients or their families into any particular choice as they approach the end of life.

> ➢ Amend Medicare laws to assure that professional counselors engaged by the

patient or family to assist them in navigating their path through these difficult waters will be reasonably compensated.

****

Discussion:

First a story, a true one, as all the best stories are. It is told by Steve Larchuk, one of the Co-authors of this book.

About ten years ago I received a call that my step father, Rodney, as dear to me as any natural father could be, had suffered a stroke and was in a hospital. Of course I dropped everything and drove to be at his bedside with Rodney's other son, my half-brother.

We found Rodney unconscious with all of the usual tubes and respirators that preserve life but unmistakably signal approaching death. His physician counseled us to be prepared for his passing, there was nothing to be done. After a few more such reports my brother and I began to refer to this doctor by the initials "DG", short for "Doom and Gloom".

After a couple of days DG was off duty. My brother and I entered Rodney's room and found a new doctor looking over the chart. We introduced ourselves and he shook our hands (which DG had never done) and told us his name. And this is the absolute truth, his name was Dr. Angel. When we asked how long our father had to live Dr. Angel seemed surprised and answered, "he will be up and walking tomorrow." And he was, living a very happy and healthy additional year.

The point of the story comes later.

During the days before the Affordable Care Act many of us were deeply involved in the Pennsylvania single payer health insurance movement. I drove all over the Commonwealth speaking to large groups and small. This included testimony before the House and Senate of the Pennsylvania Legislature and meetings with members of Congress. It took that many miles and that many speeches to distill the message down to this.

There are seven real challenges in health care reform. Six are relatively easy. The seventh is very hard. Since the first are easy we can tick them off along with the corresponding solution:

Health Care for All - Expand Medicare to all ages.

Medical Negligence - A No-Fault Compensation System.

Cost of Drugs - Extend the Patents But Require Reasonable Pricing.

Child Obesity - Establish a Curriculum of Wellness in Our Schools.

Co-Pays/Deductibles - Abolish them.

Communication - Compensate Doctors for Time Consulting.

Easy? Well, relatively easy when compared to the seventh. And the seventh is the most confounding because it blends the heart and the pocketbook mixed with guilt and fear. The seventh challenge is navigating the final six months of life.

In her beautiful book, *Final Exam – A Surgeon's Reflections on Mortality*, Dr. Pauline Chen takes us through the education of a medical student first learning to confront death, and the transition to residency and then to advanced specialty training where death becomes a matter of near routine.

She describes reaching the point in her career where she carefully excused herself from the bedside of a dying patient so friends and family could have their privacy. For a time she became an observer:

> "At the end of life the desire among patients and those around them to resolve past issues and to make things right is particularly strong ... [p]ushing for greater intervention is the seemingly natural extension of these feelings, and the treatment becomes a metaphor not only for love but of hope."

Although she never mentions the cost of end of life care Dr. Chen notes that many physicians are uncomfortable in situations where the family will not let go and costly continuing but futile treatments do little but inflict further pain and suffering. It is a price paid for a lack of preparation and acceptance that the end has come. But of course, the financial impact is significant with a large percentage of health care expenditures occurring in the last weeks of life.

Ultimately Dr. Chen graduated to the next level of her profession and became reacquainted with her humanity. Since then she has made a point to stay with the patient and their loved ones during the final moments to help them all through the transition. It is plain that not until she was able to do this did she consider herself a fully developed healer. It was her final exam.

After speaking on the topic of health care reform so many times it dawned on me that there is little government can do, and probably nothing it should do, to help the individual prepare themselves for the fate we all share. According to Dr. Chen, 90% of us will die following a long disease. It is the norm. And yet, so many of us are ill prepared when the time comes for ourselves and for our families.

Some with a strong faith in organized religion dislike the word "spirituality". It sounds to many like a superficial or lite version of faith. To those who feel that way no disrespect is intended. It is a handy word to broadly address whatever approach to philosophy or religion works for each individual.

Dying is ultimately the most singular and solitary experience of our lives and it requires the time and preparation to think it through. It also demands the will to hang on when the worst comes – the fears – the doubts – sometimes the pain - the instinct for self-preservation – the longing to agree to anything health care has to offer to purchase for ourselves or our loved ones a little more time.

Not so long ago the Sarah Palins of the World shouted down any discussion of the end of life realities with accusations of "death panels". Those intimidated by such nonsense are finally coming out from beneath the covers.

It is not a question of money, and at least this writer would oppose pressuring anyone to essentially end their own lives a little sooner by declining "heroic" measures. This is why this section starts with Rodney. Often hope is perfectly reasonable. And we all have similar stories.

But the path to making one's own decisions should start before the final diagnosis. In community, or solitarily, we must resolve these final questions so as to better navigate the last days of our lives and the lives of those who entrust to us these choices for them.

Yes, the first six challenges are relatively easy. Relatively.

"Reform of the medical liability system
Should be considered as part of a
Comprehensive response to surging medical
Malpractice premiums that endanger
Americans' access to quality medical care."
Lincoln Chafee

****

QUESTION:

Do You Support Replacing Medical Malpractice Litigation With A Better Compensation System?

Answer: Yes.

****

A Better Congress Will:

➢ Pass legislation providing for a simplified, uniform and national compensation system to assure prompt and fair financial relief to individuals who are injured by their care.

➢ Adopt laws financing the program at the Federal level and eliminate the need for physician and hospital paid medical malpractice insurance.

➢ Include in the law procedures to assure that every claim of medical error or complication is fully investigated, not to punish, but to identify patterns of mistakes and also best practices to reduce the potential for recurrence.

****

Discussion:

There appears to be considerable confusion regarding professional negligence litigation, what is typically referred to as medical malpractice. Although the details vary somewhat state to state in general a person injured due to the failure of their health care provider to exercise the required standard of care is theoretically entitled to be fully and fairly compensated for their injury.

Money to pay such a judgment typically comes from a for-profit medical malpractice insurance company which charges premiums weighted to reflect the frequency of claims and the value of such cases. Many lawyers, on both sides of these matters, and those employed as expert witnesses, make a very good living serving this medical malpractice industrial complex. They insist that the system is efficient and fair to health care providers and their patients. That is not true. Not even close.

In fact, if you believe that you are the victim of malpractice the probability of your being made 100% whole, in other words fully compensated for your pain, suffering, inconvenience, lost time from work, added medical expenses and the rest is – zero. Even with the strongest facts and the best lawyers, you will never be made whole. In fact the odds of making it to a jury award that secures to you even a 50% recovery, is about one in a hundred. It is a miserable system that substantially fails to compensate those injured by their care.

Flipping to the other side of the coin, the existing system is rightfully and understandably detested by health care professionals. They perceive it to be a grotesque lottery that threatens to inconvenience and embarrass them at best and bankrupt them at worst. As a result health care providers often try to protect themselves by practicing what is called "defensive medicine". This is the practice of managing patient care with an eye toward avoiding any possible question of oversight and therefore ordering every imaginable test, regardless of the cost or added risk to the patient.

One industry estimate is that defensive medicine accounts for 26% to 34% of the total cost of health care in the United States. That seems unlikely, but a very reasonable estimate as low as 5% translates into $125 Billion in unnecessary expense and patient inconvenience. This is a substantial sum and an inexcusable waste of money that could be better invested in actual health services.

In cases where physicians are brought into court for alleged malpractice they find they are in unfamiliar waters. Typically, under peer review required in many hospitals, the questions are asked by fellow professionals who understand the science and the possibilities and limitations of medicine. By contrast a courtroom is filled with non-medical professionals and a jury where anyone with a scintilla of medical expertise is carefully and deliberately culled lest they violate the theoretical purity of the fact finding process.

If after this trial by ordeal, excruciating for both sides and taking years, there is a finding of negligence, there will be another round of appeals consuming more time and delaying further any hope of compensation. Then, ultimately, if there is a financial recovery for the injured patient or their family, typically 50% must be surrendered to the lawyer for their fee and reimbursement of the heavy expenses incurred to bring a case to final conclusion.

A far better system has been suggested. It is called a No-Fault approach and provides a schedule of compensation for any case where a patient is made worse by their care. Instead of trying to prove a failure of care, and show that such negligence actually caused the harm complained of, instead No-

Fault provides for a rapid processing of claims regardless of blame. The amounts paid may not represent what might have eventually been achieved given a best case scenario and perfect evidence – but the awards will be fair and consistent and not subject to the substantial delays and legal fees and costs haircut that make the current system such a mockery of justice.

For the health care providers they are relieved from the fear of financial ruin but not of the obligation to participate in an investigation of the claim for the purposes of education and better management of future patients. The process is no longer geared toward blame but rather becomes more collaborative and productive. Defensive medicine will fade away replaced with a more positive practice of constant improvement in the quality of care.

Through the No-Fault system the odds of a recovery for a patient injured by their care becomes 100% with little lost to advocates or trial expenses. Traditional medical malpractice insurance is replaced with a system that ultimately costs less through the elimination of the expense and uncertainty of litigation. The courts are no longer burdened with complex medical negligence litigation and thus all other matters can move more swiftly through the system.

A Better Congress will not be afraid to confront the medical malpractice litigation insurance and litigation perpetuation lobbyists, and will instead develop and pass humane, effective and efficient reform legislation to solve the problems associated with our current car wreck of a system.

"America's health care system is in crisis Precisely because we systematically neglect Wellness and prevention."

Tom Harkin

****

QUESTION:

Should We Get Serious About a Curriculum of Wellness In Our Schools?

Answer: Yes.

****

A Better Congress Will:

Pass legislation encouraging schools across the Nation to adopt an age appropriate "Curriculum of Wellness" defined as a K through 12 commitment to educating children about their bodies, nutrition, exercise, first aid, mental health, substance abuse, care of the elderly and other life skills, all intended to elevate health awareness to the level of reading and math in importance. Congress will provide the funding required to support this program.

****

Discussion:

Americans no longer tolerate a student passing from grade to grade without regard to whether they are actually learning the basic essentials that will enable them to function as productive citizens in society. And yet, we fail to

153

seriously embrace the equally important obligation to teach these students the essentials of good health, nutrition, exercise, first aid, substance abuse avoidance, elder care, and the other components of what can be called, "A Curriculum of Wellness".

It hardly needs to be said that a child may never again use the principles of geometry once they graduate high school. But expertise in life and wellness skills will be used every day for the rest of their lives. And if used well the rewards to the student will be seen in both good heath and financial success. What could be more important or more essential? A "Core" curriculum that does not serve the whole child is unworthy of the name.

This has nothing to do with intruding on the role of the parents. During the time a child is in school the teachers are charged with assuring their students are not idle. To the contrary they should be kept active and motivated to attain the best fitness and competency in wellness that they can achieve.

Such students will perform better academically as well. There is simply no downside to this beyond the will to make it happen and reasonable funding to develop best practices and approaches.

ARTICLE FOUR

OUR ENVIRONMENT

The Questions:

Global Warming – Is it a Natural Cycle or Man Made?

Transition to Renewables – Has Government Done Enough?

What is the Future of Public Utilities?

Do Americans Have the Constitutional Right to Pollute?

Do We Worry Too Much About Clean Water?

Endangered Species – Does the System Work?

Driverless Cars: What Will Be The Impact?

"Climate change is a global problem with Grave implications: environmental, social, Economic, political, and for the distribution Of goods. It represents one of the principal Challenges facing humanity in our day."

Pope Francis

****

QUESTION:

Global Warming – Is it a Natural Cycle Or Man Made?

Answer: The debate rages but it appears to be a natural change accelerated by human activity.

****

A Better Congress Will:

> ➢ Undertake a complete investigation of the best science available to determine if it is already too late to reverse or delay the impact of global warming.

> ➢ If it is not too late then the available choices of action must be considered and where useful implemented without further delay.

> ➢ If it is too late, or if it is determined that the impact of human activity has had only negligible impact on a naturally occurring phenomenon, then Congress must plan for the inevitable effects of rising waters, shifts in weather patterns, and the challenges of climate refugees.

****

Discussion:

There are parts of the World where the effects of global warming are undeniable. The polar caps are the most obvious. Island nations are another. Much of the Bahamas is less than 30 feet above sea level and it is a matter of decades before many of those Islands will be uninhabitable. Elsewhere in the World there are plain signs of climate change. Often what is revealed is that this has all happened before, long before humans were in a position to influence the process.

What appears to be different is the rapidity of the change. Whether humans are responsible for that, or could do anything about it if we wanted to, is a valid question. As in all things a sober consideration of the facts is required. And, again as always, those in a position to act must resist the temptation to just "do something" regardless of the potential costs or unintended consequences.

Another perfectly fair question is whether there is a point to one group of countries incurring substantial economic disruption to reduce its contributions to greenhouse gas emissions while another group aggressively does just the opposite? Add to that the other equally valid question of whether a nation that contributes a disproportionate share of world wide pollution has the moral right to lecture others?

Of all of the questions, and of all of the competing and conflicting answers, the most urgent is this. Is it already too late to change the path we are on? If dramatic measures were taken, immediately, what difference would it make? Certainly efforts to reduce pollution in our cities and waterways always make sense independent of climate change issues, but will it also slow global warming?

This is the question Congress must answer before any others. If we can feasibly and confidently act to slow the pace of environmental change then we should be doing it. But if there is nothing to be done then Government needs to be planning for the consequences and stop quibbling about the cause.

"Don't get me wrong: I love nuclear energy! It's just that I prefer fusion to fission. And it Just so happens that there's an enormous Fusion reactor safely banked a few million Miles from us. It delivers more than we could Ever use in just about 8 minutes. And it's Wireless!`

William McDonough

****

QUESTION:

Transition to Renewables – Has Government Done Enough?

Answer: Not nearly enough.

****

A Better Congress Will:

➢ Adopt a coherent energy policy that stimulates research, development, and deployment of sustainable and clean energy generation and storage systems.

➢ Pass legislation supporting the expansion of a smart grid capable of better managing available energy resources and routing them to the best point of consumption.

➢ Continue to fund the United States Export Import Bank loan and credit guarantee programs to help American energy innovators export our renewable energy systems throughout the World.

****

Discussion:

In 2009 this writer constructed a three bedroom residence using state of the art solar electric modules with the objective of offsetting close to 100% of the power requirements of the home with electricity generated from sunlight. Back then the wholesale cost of solar panels was $3.80 per watt. So the cost of the solar panels alone for a 5.4 kilowatt (5,400 watts) system was over $20,000. In 2015 the price for the same size system is about $3,500.

In other words, the wholesale price of solar electric panels has dropped over 80% in six years. During that same time the cost of wind generated electricity has also declined, although not quite as dramatically. As a result most of the new electricity generation brought on line these days in the United States is renewable solar or wind.

As of this writing, according to the U.S. Energy Information Association, solar, wind, and geo-thermal sources account for about 5.5% of total electricity generation. This compares to 39% from coal, 27% from natural gas, 19% from nuclear and 6% from hydroelectric sources. Only 1% of the electricity generated in the United States comes from petroleum. That is to say, the United States can boast that it is fundamentally self-sufficient for electricity generation of which about 12% comes from renewable sources, so far.

Growth of solar and wind generation has been substantially encouraged by Federal tax policy that in the early years included 30% cash grants under the now expired Section 1603 program. Almost as useful have been the investment tax credits and accelerated depreciation incentives that are currently scheduled to substantially sunset at the end of 2016. As large solar and wind projects take years to plan, fund, permit and build this 2016 deadline is already beginning to impact further development. By the end of 2015 very few new projects will be in planning.

Does Congress care? It is perfectly rational to argue that the incentives were a temporary carrot to induce business to undertake the technical and financial risks represented by early sustainable energy projects. And, it has worked. Large solar and wind farm installations have been constructed and thanks to this demand the cost of solar panels, for example, has dropped.

Which leads those opposed to continuing these incentives to ask, what more do the environmentalists want? Why, many ask, should taxpayers continue to subsidize energy technology that cannot otherwise compete with other home grown fuels such as coal and natural gas?

Those advocating green technology have a lot to say in response. First, all energy generators are subsidized one way or the other. Second, it is not comparing apples to apples unless the environmental impact of mining, transporting, and then combusting, coal, oil, and natural gas is considered. Third, coal, oil, and natural gas are finite resources. Fourth, small solar electric and wind systems offer an opportunity for business and homeowners to generate all or some of their own electricity thus granting to them some independence from utilities while at the same time lessening the burden on utility power grids.

Until the past five years a standard objection to solar and wind has been that they are by nature intermittent sources of power. The sun and winds are fickle and constantly changing. Where such renewable generators represent a small fraction of the total amount of electricity in a utility grid the capricious spikes and drops of electricity from solar and wind generators can be covered by small adjustments at large fossil fuel plants.

This percentage of grid energy represented by renewables is referred to in the industry as "penetration". And for years it has been predicted that 20% penetration of intermittent generators represents the limits of what existing fossil fuel based utility systems can tolerate. Anything more, and sudden weather events result in overwhelming surges or drops in voltage with resultant outages.

And this is, or at least was, true. The intermittency of solar and wind resources has been a self-limiting factor in its expansion. A dramatic example of this has been seen where large wind farms have been taken out of production from time to time because the wind has been too strong thus overwhelming the grids into which the wind generated electricity was being fed. Similar issues arise with solar. It is common for production from a solar facility to drop 80% in one second due to a passing cloud, and then spike up again as soon as the cloud passes.

During the past five years however the ability to store the energy created by solar and wind generators has dramatically improved. Elon Musk through his Tesla organization is already constructing a massive plant in Nevada (not Asia thank you) to manufacture on a mass production scale lithium-ion batteries. These will be used in Tesla vehicles and also in homes, starting with

Musk's Solar City affiliate. More importantly, mass production means the cost of storage is also reduced to the point where utility scale energy storage is possible.

Regardless of the technology used, batteries act as a sponge soaking up excess electricity when the sun is strong or the winds are blowing and then releasing the stored energy when necessary to compensate for changes in the weather. Penetration becomes irrelevant since the energy storage acts as a shock absorber assuring that the grid never feels the effect of ever changing solar and wind conditions.

Tesla's product is just one of a wave of technologies that were developed in part with the funds made available by the American Recovery Act of 2009. Thank you Mr. President and Congress for that shot in the arm. It is now possible to increase renewable penetration to 50% and even to 100%, as we transition over time away from fossil fuels.

It is conceivable that this could happen incrementally without continuing Federal incentives. But that is unlikely. Energy storage has made substantial strides but the industry will die without an assured pipeline of projects and predictable demand sufficient to comfort investors to develop the manufacturing capabilities required to meet that market.

For this reason a Better Congress will pass long term tax policies and other incentives that will allow business to plan a decade in advance. Likewise, tax breaks will help the average small business or homeowner make investments in self-generated electricity with all of the advantages that entails.

"Rooftop solar is the first true form of Competition that utilities have ever faced, And that is why they're attacking it."

Lynn Jurich

****

QUESTION:

What is the Future of Public Energy Utilities?

Answer: Public utilities will generate ever decreasing amounts of electricity. Instead they will become the distribution provider over a smart and secure grid carrying electricity generated by a diversified group of private, public, and millions of individual residential generators. They will also need to harden their assets and systems against physical and cyber threats.

****

A Better Congress Will:

➢ Pass legislation favoring the orderly transition of electric utilities toward cleaner and renewable energy production methods.

➢ Require utilities to fully cooperate with the efforts of home owners and business to generate their own electricity through net metering or cash credit mechanisms that enable a consumer to recover the cost of their investment in a reasonable time.

➢ Adopt incentives to encourage utilities to harden themselves against physical and cyber- attack.

****

Discussion:

Utilities, even those owned privately or by shareholders, are unique in American business. By law they are granted monopolies over certain geographic areas and thus need not compete with others. This avoids the disorderly consequences of multiple distribution lines serving the same population. However, the tradeoff is that the utilities are closely regulated as to price, service standards, and profitability.

By and large the population of a service area ceded to a utility is at the mercy of that business and government regulators for the quality and price of the service. Being "off the grid" has for generations been considered an eccentric act of antisocial behavior reserved for hermits and survivalists. But that is all changing.

During the past ten years many average Americans have begun to resist the notion that they are captive to utilities. With the rapid decline in the cost of solar electric panels, wind turbines, batteries, and energy management devices, more homes have become partially or completely self-sufficient. Businesses too have moved in the direction of self-generated electricity, or at least advanced power management, to reduce their dependence on sometimes unreliable utility electricity and ever increasing costs.

To those who have experienced it, there is nothing quite as satisfying as watching your utility meter spin backwards when your solar panels are creating more electricity than you can use. For the consumer it is liberating and thrilling. For the utility, not so much.

As utilities are guaranteed a reasonable profit, the reduction in paying customers, or at least a reduction in how much power they consume, represents a loss of top line revenue. Without the same income the fixed costs of the utility consume a greater percentage of the available cash resulting in lower profits. Regulators are then petitioned for rate increases to restore revenue and profits. Higher rates then drive more customers to reduce consumption or to disconnect completely with the benefit of self-generated electricity. Of course, this further reduces the sale of utility generated electricity, which reduces revenue, which reduces profits, and so forth and so on.

At first this was a nuisance for utilities, nothing more. But now, especially in places with abundant sun and wind, such as Hawaii, California, and Arizona, so many consumers are pulling the plug that the financial model underpinning the utility scheme is threatened. The trend is now expanding north and east as the cost of self-sufficiency competes with the cost of dependence.

Meanwhile, consumers unable to employ the strategy of installing solar panels, apartment renters for example, find themselves forced to pay higher rates for electricity to make up for the lost revenue from those leaving the system. So the less well off are subsidizing those with the wherewithal to become self sufficient.

Although not as dramatic as consumers going off the grid completely, there is a parallel phenomenon with more efficient appliances, installation of LED lights, and reduced water consumption. These virtuous behaviors again have an adverse effect on utilities which have made massive capital investments to support predicted long term consumer demand that is fading, or at least slowing.

Layered on top of this are the threats represented by potential terrorism and cyber attacks. As is readily apparent, the distribution systems for utilities, and, to an unsettling extent their generation plants and reservoirs, are vulnerable to physical sabotage by the most amateurish of criminals.

Recently California experienced incidents of individuals shooting at transformers. Is this sport, extortion, or something more worrisome?

Cyber attacks are a larger problem. As utilities seek to become more efficient they entrust more of their operations to computer controls and Internet connectivity. With each such evolution to centralized technology the ability of an attacker to cause massive disruptions are likewise enhanced. Dealing with this has created another expense for utilities that they seek to pass on to the consumers. Increased rates stimulate lower demand, with the natural death spiral of consequences as noted above.

This is a National problem. Congress must, sooner or later, adopt legislation that will enable utilities and local authorities to evolve to a new model to assure the continuing availability of the shared utility services upon which we rely for public health, safety and economic stability.

*"We shall never understand the natural
Environment until we see it as a living
Organism. Land can be healthy or sick,
Fertile or barren, rich or poor, lovingly
Nurtured or bled white. Our present
Attitudes and laws governing the ownership
And use of land represent an abuse of the
Concept of private property.... Today you can
Murder land for private profit. You can leave
The corpse for all to see and nobody calls
The cops."*

Paul Brooks

****

QUESTION:

Do Americans Have the Constitutional Right to Pollute?

Answer: No.   We have just one planet and we need to take care of it.

****

A Better Congress Will:

Build on the environmental protection movement that since the 1970s had dramatically reversed the process of polluting our environment for temporary economic gain.

****

Discussion:

In an episode of the very popular cable television show "Mad Men", a 1960's era advertising executive takes his family out into country where they have a beautiful and relaxing picnic in a perfect meadow. When they are finished they shake out their blanket and leave a mountain of trash behind. It is shocking, not because it is fiction, but because it is history. Before the golden days of the environmental movement of the 1970's it was common for us to treat the World as a trash can and open sewer.

It would be hard to imagine anyone leaving such a mess fifty years later. But it has been only fifty years. It is comforting to know we can change, for the better.

Yet we see in American politics a worrisome acceptance that the earth is secondary to the interests of business. Republican candidates for president use the Environmental Protection Agency as a punching bag for cheap applause. Expanded rules to include streams that run seasonally within the protection of the Clean Water Act have been met in Congress with efforts to defund the Agency to prevent enforcement.

It would seem that some businesses believe they have a Constitutional right to pollute. Health and safety do not count. Clean water is irrelevant. Future generations, can just take care of themselves.

Standing up for the environment these days takes courage – it should be the other way around.

"Here is your country. Cherish these
Natural wonders, cherish the natural
Resources, cherish the history and romance
As a sacred heritage, for your children and
Your children's children. Do not let selfish
Men or greedy interests skin your country of
Its beauty, its riches or its romance."

Theodore Roosevelt

****

QUESTION:

Do We Worry Too Much About Clean Water?

Answer: No, not enough.

****

A Better Congress Will:

➢ Support the EPA's efforts to expand Clean Water Act protection to include the 60% of streams that only flow seasonally or after rains. These streams and adjacent wetlands are a vital part of area our environment.

➢ Investigate chemical hydraulic fracturing practices to determine whether Federal laws and regulations are required to assure that ground water is protected.

****

179

Discussion:

Assuring that Americans have abundant and clean water became a matter of Federal concern with the passage of the Clean Water Act in 1972.

This writer remembers when in the 1960's the rivers that define Pittsburgh were so polluted that one did not even touch the water as the stench would cling. Thanks to the Clean Water Act, and the political will to stand up to business and even municipal polluters, the health of the Allegheny, Monongahela, and Ohio Rivers of Western Pennsylvania improved to the point that by 2005 Pittsburgh hosted the "Bassmaster Classic" fishing competition with anglers from 22 states fishing the rivers and catching bass.

Without the courage of the Democratic Congress in the early 1970's, with the cooperation of the Republican administration then in power, the Clean Water Act would not have become law. Such forward thinking legislation could never pass the current Congress. Which is more than just a shame.

In May 2015, the Environmental Protection Agency issued final rules expanding the definition of protected waters to include the 60% of streams that only flow seasonally or after rains. What is surprising is that for so long these streams, and associated wetlands, have not been considered to be within the protection of the Act. These Rules were issued after lengthy debate and the usual expected knee jerk opposition.

There are some Members of the Republican/Tea Party controlled Congress, including some representing areas through which the great Pittsburgh Rivers flow, with very short memories and strong ties to industry that trump their commitment to the People and the environment. They disassociate themselves with the Republicans of forty-five years ago who they disdain as being too liberal. The current claimants to the once great Republican heritage have little commitment to protecting the environment.

To the business-above-all Republican/Tea Party coalition any expansion of clean water protection is unacceptable. They simply do not care about the 60% of streams and wetlands that remain at the mercy of polluters. Is this representative of the People? Hardly.

Nor does our current Congress have any interest in the permanent damage being done to underground water resources and aquifers due to reckless chemical hydraulic fracking. To those with any direct experience with property owners who have leased their gas rights to developers, there is clear evidence that industry promises regarding protection of underground water have not been honored. Rural land owners who have for generations relied upon well water are finding their wells dry, or tainted, once drilling operations have begun. This is another area that demands courageous intervention by those who care about water.

Last, Californians understand as well as anyone the consequences of poor water management. The drought there, and the recurring droughts in Oklahoma and elsewhere, remind us that clean water is our most precious resource. Congress should act accordingly.

"What is the use of a house if you haven't Got a tolerable planet to put it on?"

Henry David Thoreau

****

QUESTION:

Endangered Species – Does the System Work?

Answer: Not perfectly – we need to do better.

****

A Better Congress Will:

> ➢ Resist political pressure to weaken or abandon our National commitment to preserving the diversity of life.

> ➢ Undertake an examination of existing law to determine if those who are adversely impacted by the discovery of protected species on their land are being fairly compensated. This addresses the question of whether restricting the otherwise lawful use of property to protect the general interests of the People constitutes a "taking" under the 5th Amendment that requires payment just as the taking of land for a highway requires fair compensation.

****

Discussion:

All one has to say is "Spotted Owl" and eyes roll. Two words reflect the frustration that many feel about the perceived excesses of the Endangered Species Act of 1973. More positively, one can say "Bald Eagle", and see a more sympathetic response.

As a businessman this writer has experience with the short end of the environmental stick in a somewhat ironic way. As a developer of utility scale solar systems that substantially reduce greenhouse gases and dependence on imported petroleum one would think we might get some consideration when it comes to getting approval from environmental watchdogs. Wrong.

Our company had secured an option on 40 acres of land where we planned to build a large solar electric plant. As part of the permitting process we undertook the required environmental survey. The report came back that there were no species of plant or animals on the protected list. However, the local environmental permitting officials refused our application due to the presence of a plant species that in their opinion was "threatened". This was insufficient under law to block our project, but we would have been required to go into court and litigate for years.

So we moved on to another site. Certainly we lost money but not so much as to worry about. But the land owner from whom we were going to lease the land not only lost the deal with us, but has essentially lost the value of the land for any purpose, forever. This is unfair. And it is the sort of government action that frustrates business and property owners.

This land had been in the same family for generations and long before the Endangered Species Act. The owners had not polluted it or conducted any sort of business on it at all. But through the whim of a few government regulators the value of the land had been substantially reduced in the name of the American People. Had the land been taken for a highway or other more obvious public use the owners would have received compensation. But not in this instance, and that is wrong.

Certainly we have a duty to identify and protect endangered species. But in the process regulators also have a duty to appreciate and respect the interests of property owners, developers, and taxpayers to apply the law evenly, predictably, and fairly. In the real world, having the right to challenge in court abusive or incorrect acts, or sometimes governmental refusals to act, is a completely inadequate remedy. Litigation is too expensive, takes too long, and the results are too uncertain. Disqualification of property for development as a matter of public policy is as much a taking as any other act of *eminent domain.*

We do not need to repeal the Act, abolish the EPA, or take any other excessive steps. But businessmen know that the law, and the way it is currently administered, requires review and improvement. A Better Congress will do that.

"Some Google employees have Their self-driving vehicles take them To work. These car robots don't look Like something from 'The Jetsons'; the Driverless features on these cars are a Bunch of sensors, wires, and software. This technology works."

Tyler Cowen

****

QUESTION:

Driverless Cars: What Will Be The Impact?

Answer: Cleaner air, safer roads, lower cost for transportation of freight and people - and massive employment disruption. A taste of the good and the bad of robotics.

****

A Better Congress Will:

> ➢ Exercise its authority under the Commerce Clause of the Constitution to remove barriers to the adoption of driverless technologies with America leading the way in this industry.

> ➢ Anticipate and plan for massive unemployment among professional drivers, technicians, insurance adjusters, and repair shops.

****

Discussion:

As we watch the headlong development of driverless cars and trucks we are being told that by 2025 these will be commonplace. Quite likely the most immediate use of the fleet of driverless cars will be as taxis. This is because there will be some resistance of the average consumer to make the leap to driverless cars. But the advantages for the short term shared ride industry are numerous. Here is a list to name the most obvious:

1. Perfect efficiency – no down time except to refuel (recharge?) and for maintenance. The vehicles can operate 24 hours a day.

2. Safety – driverless cars "refuse to crash" – in other words they are the ultimate in defensive drivers assuming and anticipating inadvertent driving from human driven vehicles and communicating with other driverless cars to resolve conflicts without resorting to road rage.

3. Fuel management – driverless cars will calculate the most efficient route taking into account weather, time of day, the communal shared experience of the fleet, internet reported accidents and breakdowns, and construction.

4. Never lost – GPS management assures every car knows where it is going.

5. Friend to Law Enforcement – connected to face recognition software these driverless cars can quickly help law enforcement find and capture persons of interest. If necessary a signal can disable the car at a safe location where law enforcement is waiting. Plus, no law enforcement time is wasted writing tickets for moving violations.

6. Environmentally Friendly – assuming most of these driverless cars will eventually be electric, compressed natural gas or hydrogen, the amount of exhaust emissions will be dramatically reduced.

So, cool, right? Except for the massive employment disruption.

Ride sharing innovator Uber has seen this coming and is now deeply invested in developing driverless technologies. As summarized above, driverless transportation will trump human driven vehicles on just about any metric.

Driverless taxis will change the way we live. With greater efficiency and reliability, plus 24 hour up time, driverless cabs will reduce the need for individuals to own their own cars which means fewer car sales and all of the economics driven by car manufacture, sales, insurance, repair and fuel. Translation: fewer jobs.

Take the next logical step to long haul trucking and hundreds of thousands of long haul drivers are out of work. Exactly what will these displaced men and women do? Somehow we need to anticipate and plan for this dramatic transition – not wait for it to happen and then hope we can react.

Many will benefit from these changes but the disadvantages cannot fairly fall on so few, so quickly, and without a plan for what follows. A Better Congress will see such disruptions coming and do what it can to eliminate barriers to new technologies while at the same time embracing the needs of those who get caught in the middle.

ARTICLE FIVE
PRIVACY AND PERSONAL LIBERTY

The Questions:

*After 9/11 Do Americans Still Have a
Right to Privacy?*

Do You Support Marriage Equality?

Is the Right to Bear Arms Absolute?

*Do Women Have the Liberty to
Control Their Bodies?*

*Time to Reconsider the Equal Rights
Amendment for Women?*

*Mass Incarceration – Criminal Justice?
Or Injustice?*

*Does Religious Freedom Include the
Right to Discriminate Against Those Who Do Not
Share My Religious Values?*

"Those who surrender freedom for security
Will not have, nor do they deserve, either
One."

Benjamin Franklin

****

QUESTION:

After 9/11 Do Americans Still Have a Right to Privacy?

Answer: Americans have a right to privacy, if they have the courage to protect it.

****

A Better Congress Will:

> Adopt a "Compelling and Convincing" standard when weighing proposed surveillance and data collection laws. Existing laws that cannot meet this standard should be repealed.

****

Discussion:

There are many excellent books on our loss of privacy in the wake of September 11th. One of these, *Data and Goliath: The Hidden Battle to Collect Your Data and Control Your World,* written by Bruce Schneier, is among the best. He presents the government dilemma succinctly:

That's fear talking, but it is not fear of terrorists. Its political fear of being blamed when there's a terrorist attack. The career politician wants to do everything possible, regardless of the cost, regardless of whether it actually makes anyone safer, regardless of the side effects, to avoid blame for not having done enough. This explains the post 9/11 anti-terrorism policy and much of the NSA's mass surveillance programs.

Think what you will of Senator Rand Paul, at least on the issue of personal privacy he is unafraid to speak out. As for Edward Snowden, the leaker who revealed the scope of the NSA programs, history will eventually be the judge of his claimed patriotism.

Those of us involved in the Internet industry were aware, or at least strongly suspected, that warrantless government intrusions into databases was happening on a massive scale. Shortly after September 11th it was common to receive government requests for access to database information of various groups and individuals that might be associated with terrorist activity. After the passage of the Patriot Act, official requests for help diminished.

Only the most naïve could believe this was simply because the government was no longer interested. The suspicion was the NSA or FBI no longer needed our assistance. Snowden removed any doubts on that score.

Recently France passed legislation permitting its government to engage in massive Internet and telecommunications data surveillance. This follows its version of September 11th attacks that occurred at the offices of a satirical publication and separately at a kosher grocery. One government official told NPR that he could not understand the controversy when people all over the World seem not to care at all that Facebook and others are collecting, processing and selling personal data every second of the day.

Good point. What is the difference? Actually, none. This debate is just starting.

"The Constitution promises liberty to all
Within its reach, a liberty that includes
Certain specific rights
That allow persons, within a lawful realm,
To define and express their identity."
Justice Kennedy

****

QUESTION:

Do You Support Marriage Equality?

Answer: Yes.

****

A Better Congress Will:

Adopt laws under the Commerce Clause of the Constitution to prohibit discrimination in public accommodations and otherwise in the marketplace based upon sexual orientation or sexual identification.

****

Discussion:

On June 16, 2015, by the narrowest margin of 5-4, the Supreme Court ruled that States cannot discriminate with respect to issuing civil marriage licenses on the basis of gender. It is heartening that this long awaited vindication of the rights of all

Americans has come. But it is worrisome that the views of the dissenting Members of the Court reveal how precarious the decision may be and how bitter the opposition remains.

Notwithstanding the views of the Minority of the Supreme Court, it has been with surprising speed that marriage equality has moved to the main stream. Only 12% of the members of Congress cosigned a "friend of the court" brief submitted to the Supreme Court openly and unashamedly invoking "states rights" as a basis for opposing the recognition of equal protection under the 14th Amendment to the Constitution. Those 12% are plainly out of touch with the People, and now a majority of the Supreme Court.

Soon every State and Congress will be challenged to add sexual orientation and gender identification to race, age, sex, and disability as conditions that are protected against discrimination. Given the wave of support across the political and cultural spectrum for the end of official government discrimination in marriage, it is clear that the time has finally come to expand this acceptance and forbid discrimination in commerce and housing as well.

*"We need to take a harder look at what's
Really going on. Stop trying to treat the
Symptoms and treat the cause of the
Problem. Maybe we should try a little harder
To help these kids before they feel so
Cornered that they turn into monsters."*

Aaron B. Powell

****

QUESTION:

Is the Right to Bear Arms Absolute?

Answer: None of the rights expressly reserved to
the People under the Constitution and Amendments
is absolute. But the right to bear arms is no more or
less a right reserved to the People than freedom of
speech, religion, assembly, the press, trial by jury,
privacy, and the other protections expressly stated in
the Bill of Rights.

****

A Better Congress Will:

> ➤ Avoid confusing violence generally with
> "gun violence".

> ➤ Understand that untreated mental
> illness is the principal cause of gun
> violence and a comprehensive program
> to identify and treat those afflicted is a
> national priority.

****

Discussion:

There are only a few truly hot button issues in American politics and gun rights are near the top of that list.

Many who own guns identify with the Minutemen at Concord and Lexington, frontiersmen who relied on their muskets for defense and for food, and citizen soldiers in two World Wars handed a rifle and taught to use it before they shipped out to Europe and the Pacific. To them a gun is an icon, a material affirmation of a political connection with those who established and then defended the Country in a hostile World.

Others also recall being taught by a parent how to use a gun, safely, for hunting and potentially for self defense. They recall crisp autumn days hunting with relatives. Such bonding and nostalgia are comforting to many and pleasantly at odds with the day to day demands of modern life and a disconnected society. Some also believe that they cannot count on law enforcement to be there when needed and guns are the great equalizer against those who threaten life and property.

These are related, but not identical motivations. All of these points of view are often lumped together but the politics, emotions, and fears are not the same and a set of rules acceptable to some will not necessarily be accepted by others.

If we are to assume there is some significance to the order of the Bill of Rights, the first ten Amendments to the Constitution, then the Second Amendment follows only the rights of freedom of speech, the press, assembly, petition, and religion in importance. The right to bear arms was not included in the First Amendment. It could have been, but was not. Yet it is second in order and that has to mean something. It plainly was not an afterthought.

That said, it is often debated whether the reference in the Second Amendment to a "well regulated militia" was *the* reason, or merely illustrative of the multiple reasons, supporting the right to bear arms. This is a matter of never ending discussion. Perhaps the militia language simply reflected the principal concerns of the day for frontier defense against Native American raids or southern slave revolts that at the time were a frequent occurrence throughout the Caribbean and a constant fear among the slave owning states.

Whatever the original rationale was for the Constitutional recognition of gun ownership, the courts have interpreted the right to mean that citizens in this Country may own guns for reasons beyond the maintenance of a well regulated militia. More to the point, the courts have recognized the right to bear arms is a matter of personal protection of lives and property. With limits.

What limits? Few would argue that the Second Amendment constitutionally protects the right to own artillery – although if one agrees that the people have the right to sufficient arms to protect themselves from an oppressive government then artillery would come in handy. But even the most ardent guns rights advocate would not go that far.

Where can the lines be drawn? Wherever the limitations are set they must be grounded in some compelling and rational cause and not on emotions. For those who abhor guns without condition or exception there is no middle ground. They understandably point to other industrialized nations where gun ownership is rare and the murder rate is much lower. They argue this is not mere coincidence.

Over the years we have seen horrifying orgies of violence where the perpetrators have often used guns. We refer to these events by their location: Columbine, Newtown, Aurora, Virginia Tech, Waco, Charleston, and so on as if to say by labeling the particular event we can distinguish it from the others. But really they are all the same. And it is nothing new. Older Americans will remember the sniper shooting of August 1966 when a man killed 16 and wounded 32 from his clock tower perch at the University of Texas.

A comprehensive study published by *USA Today* reports that mass killings, defined as four or more dead in a single incident, occur in the United States approximately every two weeks. Most involve guns. However the total of such deaths only represents about one percent of the cumulative homicides in the United States. Not sure exactly what to take from that, but it suggests that the media may be missing the larger story. Violence itself.

During the turmoil of the 1960s some defended the use of force against the government as consistent with American values. "Violence is as American as Apple Pie", or so it was said. And unquestionably the Nation was carved out of the wilderness and freed from the rule of the British Empire at the barrel of a gun. But violence is not unique to America. Every inhabited continent has a never ending history of violence, including most especially our friends in Europe who have dragged themselves, and us, into two World Wars in the past 100 years.

However, the relative scarcity of guns in Europe means that those tending to violence are deprived of the multiplier effect and efficiency of firearms. By design guns enhance the lethal abilities of their possessors. That is the point, and the attraction. With the use of high capacity magazines one can shoot scores of rounds without even the inconvenience of reloading.

Such devices are sometimes used in mass shootings, and their availability likely has made escape by targeted individuals more difficult. That said, seeking to pass laws restricting access to guns, high capacity magazines, and ammunition just to "do something" is irrational. Equally useless are politicians who pander to gun owners without admitting that the frequency of gun associated deaths is unique to the United States.

We should at least be able to agree that we need to address the epidemic of untreated mental illness that lies behind these mass killings. As we dissect the timelines leading up to these events there are almost always unmistakable signals that the persons pulling the trigger required treatment. Too often there were co-workers, family and neighbors who suspected danger and who could have done something, said something, but did not. Or, if they did contact authorities they have often been ignored.

There are not two sides to this debate, there are multiple sides. A Better Congress will gently but seriously initiate steps to find common ground, to rebuild trust, and to adopt truly constructive paths toward reducing all violence.

"No woman can call herself free who does Not control her own body."

Margaret Sanger

****

QUESTION:

Do Women Have the Liberty to Control Their Bodies?

Answer: Women and Men have the liberty to control their bodies. If there is a right to privacy at all, it is most applicable to decisions we make about reproduction in consultation with our physicians and as governed by our individual moral compass.

****

A Better Congress Will:

➤ Discontinue the routine addition of "Hyde Amendment" limitations on appropriations that preclude the use of Federal tax revenues for lawful medical procedures and counseling regarding reproduction.

➤ Pass legislation intended to assure full support, maintenance and education for every child born in this Country and to assure all of the pre-natal care a mother requires to assure the safe and healthful delivery of any child she chooses to bring to term.

****

Discussion:

Quite rightly every American has an opinion on the question of women's reproductive rights. At the extremes there is no room, and often no tolerance, for doubt or debate. In the broad middle there is an honest awareness that regardless of what politicians or theologians may say, it is and always has been, a matter of choice. And so it must be unless women are to be regarded as second class citizens without the right to control their own bodies.

There are societies elsewhere who at their extreme deprive women of the right to an education and otherwise limit their freedom of dress, movement, association, speech, and certainly their reproductive independence. It is an extreme, but just a difference of degree. The line cannot be drawn at some convenient point in the middle.

If Liberty means anything it means the right to make this choice without qualification, condition or intimidation by those who may disagree.

"Women who seek to be equal with Men lack ambition."

Timothy Leary

****

QUESTION:

***Is It Time to Reconsider the
Equal Rights Amendment?***

Answer: Yes.

****

A Better Congress Will:

Resubmit to the States for ratification the Equal Rights Amendment.

****

Discussion:

During the 2014 Washington Correspondent's Dinner Joel McHale noted how qualified former Secretary of State Hillary Clinton is to be president:

She has experience. She's a natural leader, and as our first female president, we can pay her 30% less!

Our lives are filled with strong women. During the past forty years they have also become the most significant part of the work force as stagnant wages have made a second family income the only way to make ends meet. A few women have made it to the CEO chair, not enough, but some.

Very few would say with a straight face that women are hired, paid or promoted on a par with men. In addition there remains a shocking continuing tolerance for sexual harassment in the workplace – which unfortunately includes the military.

In 1923, three years after ratification of the 19th amendment giving women the vote, the suffragist Alice Paul wrote this proposed Equal Rights Amendment (ERA) to secure women their full and unquestioned equality beyond merely the right to vote:

Equality of rights under the law shall not be denied or abridged by the United States or by any State on account of sex."

Her proposal was thereafter presented to every Congress from 1923 to 1972, when finally the requisite two-thirds of both the House and Senate voted for its passage. But the Amendment failed to garner the necessary three-fourths or 38 states for ratification, the effort stalled at 35 states in 1982, and by the terms of the ERA its ratification was required within ten years. Three states shy! Since then the Amendment has been introduced in every Congress to no avail. And yet the World is very different than it was in 1982.

Is the Amendment necessary or not? Many argue that the Fourteenth Amendment adopted after the Civil War guarantees all necessary rights to every citizen regardless of gender. But if that were true then the 19th Amendment recognizing women's right to vote would not have been necessary at all. It was necessary. And the ERA is as well to remove all doubt.

The simple reality is that women are not treated equally. Studies show that women are earning 77% of what men earn for the same work. April 8th is now significant as the calendar date when women no longer work for free. Men continue to occupy the vast majority of leadership positions in this country. Male dominated legislatures also persist in dictating to women what their reproductive rights should be. This is discrimination based exclusively and entirely on gender and it must end.

In an April 2014 National Press Club speech, Supreme Court Justice Ruth Bader Ginsburg stated that if she could see one amendment added to the

Constitution it would be the Equal Rights Amendment. She acknowledged that there is legislation that guarantees women's equality, but noted that legislation can be repealed or altered. "So I would like my granddaughters, when they pick up the Constitution, to see that notion – that women and men are persons of equal stature – I'd like them to see that is a basic principle of our society." Amen.

So yes, a Better Congress should vote to send the Equal Rights Amendment back to the States for ratification.

*"The fate of millions of people—indeed the
Future of the black community itself—may
Depend on the willingness of those who care
About racial justice to re-examine their basic
Assumptions about the role of the criminal
Justice system in our society."*
                                        Michelle Alexander

****

QUESTION:

*Mass Incarceration – Criminal Justice?
Or Injustice?*

Answer: Multi-year incarcerations for non-violent crimes has created a massive population of incarcerated individuals. We need to seriously rethink what we are doing and the President should not be reluctant to use his power of the pardon to more seriously address cases of excessive punishment notwithstanding the large numbers involved.

****

A Better Congress Will:

Reexamine the criminal statutes to eliminate mandatory minimum sentences and restore to the Courts their discretion to fit the sentence to the facts and with renewed emphasis on rehabilitation as a principal goal of incarceration.

****

Discussion:

With over Two Million Americans in prisons or jails the United States is the World leader in incarceration. Not an especially proud distinction.

We got this way beginning with Richard Nixon's presidential campaign in 1968 when he sought to differentiate his platform by promising a war on crime. Which is to say a war against minorities who had responded angrily to the murder of Martin Luther King, Jr. This was part of the famous "Southern Strategy" which was intended to pull states of the old Confederacy over to the Republican column. And it worked. Nixon won by one of the narrowest margins in American history.

This later dovetailed with the claim from law and order minded politicians, each trying to outdo the other on the new issue of crime, that the Courts were being too lenient and that mandatory minimums would assure long sentences. Judges lost the power to tailor the punishment to the particular circumstances of the crime and the potential rehabilitation of the person convicted. Soon any notion that prison was also intended to do more than punish drifted away.

Those politicians appalled by this evolving harshness in sentencing dared not speak out lest they be branded as soft on crime. In 1988, Michael Dukakis lost a large early lead in the presidential election polls when Republicans used the improvident early release of Willy Horton and Dukakis's opposition to capital punishment as proof he was unfit to serve. Criminals were not a constituency that mattered. As a result sentences became longer and sometimes reflected an irrational bias against minorities.

Some progress has been made in the reform of drug laws to eliminate the plainly racially weighted sentences for crack cocaine versus its powder version. But there are still many in prison serving unduly harsh sentences for non-violent crimes. Old sentences under obsolete guidelines have not been addressed.

Every president has the Constitutional power to pardon or commute sentences of those convicted of crimes against the United States. This power was originally intended, and used, to address the potential harshness of a system that in the 1700's had little subtlety. With the power of the pardon presidents could intercede to prevent miscarriages of justice or reward good behavior.

Our president can, and should, order a case by case review of every person currently incarcerated in the Federal system for non-violent offenses and issue pardons or commutations as necessary to address situations where an injustice has been done or where there are other compelling grounds. Not a few here and there, as has happened so far in 2015, but potentially thousands of Americans should be granted sensible clemency reducing their terms to more reasonable durations.

States should likewise be encouraged to review their laws to weigh whether the legitimate goal of public safety has been lost in the smoke of law and order politics. Given the cost of incarceration it makes little sense to imprison anyone for a day longer than justice requires.

Looking forward, Congress should restore to the judiciary its discretionary function. This will provide the Courts with the ability to more precisely fit the punishment to the crime. Our judges should again be trusted with this power as they once were.

Those who advance the cause of justice are not soft on crime – they are strong on common sense.

*"I believe a Christian muffler shop owner
Should have the same right to refuse service
To a gay couple, as a gay lifeguard has to
Refuse service to a drowning Christian."*

Quentin R. Bufogle

****

QUESTION:

Does Religious Freedom Include the Right to Discriminate In Commerce or Housing Against Those Who Do Not Share My Religious Values?

Answer: Everyone has the right to act as they will within the privacy of their home, their place of worship and in their own hearts and minds. But in the shared world of public contact and commerce discrimination based upon religion or sexual orientation and gender identification is inconsistent with American values.

****

A Better Congress Will:

Amend the Civil Rights laws to better confirm that discrimination in Interstate Commerce and housing on the basis of religion or sexual orientation and gender identification is unlawful just as is discrimination based on gender, race, age and disability.

****

Discussion:

By the slimmest of margins the Supreme Court has ruled that states may not discriminate in the issuing of marriage licenses on account of gender. With that widely celebrated ruling the nation moved a little closer to the equality guaranteed to all through the 14th Amendment. But not all are happy with the decision as they see it as another example of Federal government intrusion.

Such is how it has always been with race, sex, age and disability – all of which required Federal laws to force the last hold outs to end discrimination in business and housing. And those laws have substantially succeeded. Refusing service or accommodation to a racial minority would now be unthinkable throughout most of the Country, and it would be unlawful everywhere.

Although we seem to be moving as a society with sudden and surprising swiftness to a similar standard of equality and fairness with regard to sexual orientation and gender identification, there remain individuals, and groups, who contend that their right to religious freedom is a valid basis to discriminate against those who live a lifestyle deemed inconsistent with that faith. This is nothing new. In the past personal religious doctrine and philosophies have been used to justify discrimination. We are past that.

Ours is a pluralistic and tolerant society. Even more than mere tolerance is our evolution to full hearted acceptance of diversity. It is one of our strengths. And it is part of our political fabric that has made it possible for so many of different backgrounds, races, and faiths to live and work together in harmony.

Intolerance on the grounds of sexual orientation or gender identification in business and housing is inconsistent with our values. Discriminate, if you must in your hearts, your homes and even in your places of worship. But in business and housing such intolerance is not the American way.

ARTICLE SIX

EDUCATION

The Questions:

Are Brick and Mortar Schools Obsolete?

Can We Trust Primary Education to
The Lowest Bidder?

Should Vocational Training or College be Free?

How Do We Deal With A Trillion Dollars in
Existing Student Loan Debt?

Does the Department of Education
Serve a Purpose?

STEM or Humanities – Must We Choose?

Why Are Some Schools So Much Better
Than Others?

*"Every time you stop a school, you will have
To build a jail. What you gain at one end
You lose at the other. It's like feeding a dog
On his own tail. It won't fatten the dog."*

Mark Twain

****

QUESTION:

Are Brick and Mortar Schools Obsolete?

Answer: No, but Internet based learning is a valuable tool to enhance learning and enrich the time spent in the classroom.

****

A Better Congress Will:

> ➤ Enact laws that assure that every American student has reasonable access to the Internet and a portable device that gets them there.

> ➤ Provide funding for fact based studies testing the value and effectiveness of remote learning as a stand alone education strategy and also as an adjunct to classroom instruction.

****

Discussion:

Given the cost of brick and mortar schools and staff it is tempting to imagine leveraging the power of the Internet to enable students to receive all, or at least some, of their education on line. Of course this is already happening in small numbers as parents are experimenting with cyber schools as a supplement or principal tool for home schooling.

Diana Ravitch in *Reign of Errors – The Hoax of the Privatization Movement and the Danger to America's Public Schools,* engages in a thorough and complex discussion of the problems with public education and examines the myriad of solutions to cure what might be wrong. One of those proposed solutions is cyber education as well as charter schools for all students. She acknowledges that cyber education has its place with the highly motivated student whose parents provide valuable support and guidance that might otherwise be missing from the absence of a guiding teacher.

She also acknowledges cyber education's usefulness for the student who is unable to attend public school due to physical limitations or the student whose life is currently dedicated to another pursuit such as Olympic training. But she does not see it as the panacea that for-profit education organizations claim it to be. For Dr. Ravitch and others, the jury is still out on the effectiveness of both cyber and charter school education.

She also defends public education as the cornerstone of our democracy with our need for a well-educated electorate. "The central purpose of education is to prepare everyone to assume the rights and responsibilities of citizenship in a democracy." This mission removes public education from the realm of consumer good to a public responsibility. And the brick and mortar school house remains a part of that responsibility.

As with most things relating to education the answer is likely an individual one. Some students may do better with a customized program of remote learning. Others may perform very poorly without the social experience of learning with others or the competition that can spur one on to try harder to excel. Whichever way it goes ultimately all of our children end up in the same pool and they need to swim.

Americans are not stingy when it comes to education. We pay what it takes. But the cost and the result provoke a fairly constant questioning of whether the money is being well spent. This is especially irksome to those without children who end up subsidizing the families that do. It is perfectly reasonable to demand accountability given the cost and the importance of a quality education.

What is missing for decision makers is completely reliable data upon which to make these calls. One group advocates aggressive testing to score the effectiveness of schools and even individual teachers. Others disagree claiming that such high stakes testing warps the curriculum toward simply meeting the goals established by the test makers. Where the tests are not personalized to the student or useful beyond evaluating the school itself, parents have been known to keep their children home rather than expose them to a seemingly useless testing experience.

As this is being written there are bills in Congress addressing No Child Left Behind. Although the Senate version has considerable bipartisan support the House bill is quite contentious. The good news is that at least there is some discussion and there seems to be no serious movement yet to close schools and replace them with on-line instruction. That is for the best.

"We've seen what can happen when we Entrust a basic human right to market Forces. While innovation and discovery have Emerged from private enterprise, the Distribution of the benefits of progress has Been immorally inequitable."

Steve Nelson

****

QUESTION:

Can We Trust Primary Education To the Lowest Bidder?

Answer: No.

****

A Better Congress Will:

> ➢ Continue to incentivize local communities to innovate to discover what strategies work best for their students.

> ➢ Discourage the use of competitive bidding and outsourcing of teaching to for-profit commercial vendors.

****

Discussion:

There are many books on education most of which seem determined to frighten the American people and incline them toward a privatization of education on the theory that somehow a properly incentivized cook can make a better stew with fewer ingredients. Given the billions of dollars on the table one can hardly blame American business for wanting a slice of that pie and telling school boards what they want to hear.

For those looking for a more credible analysis, and fewer food metaphors, Diane Ravitch's book, *Reign of Error – The Hoax of the Privatization Movement and the Danger to America's Public Schools* is a good place to start. The average American is ill equipped to follow the debate over Common Core, No Child Left Behind, Race to the Top, National Assessment of Educational Progress, high stakes testing and so forth, but Dr. Ravitch does a good job of explaining where these programs have come from and the (usually) good intentions behind them.

Plainly the author has a point of view, and pulls no punches, but she is clearly an expert on the subject and demands that decisions about education be based on facts and not emotion. Ultimately her point is that public schools take their students as they find them and each child needs and deserves individual attention.

Of course it is seductive to hear about school choice, vouchers, "money follows the child" teacher accountability – it all sounds so reasonable. But is it a cherry picking exercise where the money flows away from public education and to commercial enterprises that actually perform no better but do a better job on pubic relations? Can we test our way to a better system? This is not an academic discussion. It involves real students and real tax dollars that are already stretched. A vigorous debate is a good thing, but a never ending and increasingly bitter back and forth accomplishes little – we need to make some decisions.

We also need to address the perception that the Federal government is being heavy handed, manipulating funding, all in a top down imposition of questionable curriculum and standards, heavily dependent on testing, as a means to raise scores and achievement. Is there any truth to it? Why is there so much fist shaking and demands that the Department of Education be abolished?

Whatever the truth may be it seems unlikely that MBA school type solutions are going to work. What does work is investing in our children as early in their development as possible to assure they are receiving the nutrition, health care, and safe environment they need to allow their minds and bodies to grow and be ready for learning. This is why there is justifiable emphasis on pre-school programs.

Once in elementary school and beyond students need well trained professionals who have mastered the art and science of teaching. Good teachers are worth the money. Schools should also be an oasis of safety with a broad curriculum of arts and science to enrich the soul as well as preparing the student for further education and employment.

Finally, and equally important is a commitment to developing the ability of each student to manage their own bodies. There is sufficient time in the day for every child to engage in some level of physical fitness along with class work focusing on nutrition, first aid, the basics of anatomy and physiology, and the special needs of our elders. This sort of commitment to the student is unlikely to be achieved through competitive bidding.

"A system of general instruction, which Shall reach every description of our citizens, From the richest to the poorest, as it was the Earliest, so will it be the latest, of all the Public concerns in which I shall permit Myself to take an interest."

Thomas Jefferson

****

QUESTION:

Should Vocational Training or College be Free?

Answer: Not free, but realistically financed in a fashion that makes such additional learning affordable without crushing student debt.

****

A Better Congress Will:

Reinvent the student loan system to provide the means for any student willing to work hard to attend vocational and college programs while structuring the repayment program to accommodate the limited means of the young graduate.

****

Discussion:

President Obama recently floated the idea of free Community College for every American. Of course the Republican/Tea Party coalition running Congress is unlikely to take such an idea seriously as it would involve a perceived expansion of government when they are determined to shrink government to the point of complete irrelevance. Beyond such predictable knee jerk opposition there is a reasonable concern about the fairness of such a subsidy without some reasonable obligation to reimburse taxpayers for their investment.

If one takes seriously the notion that every American should have the opportunity to rise as high and go as far as their talents and character can take them, then all barriers to more advanced training and education should be removed, or at least lowered. Given the cost of higher education, including the room, board, books and living expenses involved, this is a major investment.

Many still see a liberal arts education as a worthwhile pursuit in order to enhance one's ability to think critically and engage with the world and navigate its complexities. Others see college as only a means to an end, the end being a higher paying job. There should be room in the discussion about higher education for both pursuits.

As is discussed elsewhere in this book our young people are graduating from advanced programs with crushing debt. Meanwhile the opportunities are fewer in the post-Recession World and wages remain far behind. Some steps have been taken already to help reduce the debt load or make payments more manageable. But more needs to be done. This is part of the critical strategy to help revive the Middle Class.

It is also vital that we do what is required to make sure that students graduating from high school have the tools necessary to succeed at the advanced vocational or college level. The freshman year at college has to be more than just "13th grade". We also need to reconsider whether the traditional four years of college is really necessary. Stronger two year programs can provide the training required to fill many positions.

A Better Congress will try to get past the politics and emotions and find a path that works for everyone.

*"By making college unaffordable and
Student loans unbearable, we risk deterring
Our best and brightest from pursuing higher
Education and securing a good-paying job."*
                                        Mark Pocan

****

QUESTION:

How Do We Deal With A Trillion Dollars In Existing Student Loan Debt?

Answer: This debt is an anchor around the necks of the Middle Class. We need to establish a Federal Education Bank, sponsored and capitalized by the Federal Reserve, to refinance all existing student debt to structure affordable payments at the same interest rates that Wall Street banks pay.

****

A Better Congress Will:

Pass legislation creating a Federal Education Bank, capitalized by the Federal Reserve, which will refinance 100% of this debt on payment schedules that students can afford and at the same interest rates that Wall Street Banks pay.

****

Discussion:

In August 2013, Forbes published an alarming report entitled, *"How the $1.2 Trillion*

College Debt Crisis is Crippling Students, Parents and the Economy". Quoting statistics from The Institute for College Access and Success, as well as the Consumer Financial Protection Bureau, the article stated that individual student debt averages $26,600. This might be a manageable sum except that the job market remains soft and stagnant wages are making this burden too much to bear. As this debt is guaranteed by, or owed to, the Federal Government it also has the additional negative effect of adding to the National Debt.

A review of the history of this challenge shows a blizzard of proposals and suggestions. A leading voice in this is Massachusetts Senator Elizabeth Warren who has raised the student debt plight of 40 Million Americans as a barrier to financial recovery. Among her ideas she has suggested lowering interest rates to the same rate Wall Street Banks pay for Federal Reserve funds, but the idea has been narrowly derailed by a Republican/Tea Party filibuster. Another example of the dysfunctional Senate.

This lowered interest rate should be part of a greater solution when blended with lessons learned from the Great Recession.

Faced with borrowing trillions of dollars from other nations, or from the private sector, to cover the historic Federal deficit caused by the Great Recession, we ultimately simply created more money to cover it. Quantitative Easing, and similar aggressive measures by the Federal Reserve, created trillions of dollars through a few strokes of a computer keyboard. This was what was used to cover U.S. Treasury securities and what made it unnecessary for the Treasury to drain all of the available liquidity out of the International banking system to cover our recovery spending.

Without Quantitative Easing, interest rates would have skyrocketed as commercial borrowers and consumers would have had to compete with their own government for money. But this did not happen thanks to Quantitative Easing. And therein is a lesson useful for addressing student debt.

What we learned, to the surprise and relief of many, was that the creation of huge amounts of digital money did not result in raging inflation. To the contrary inflation has remained at remarkably low levels throughout. Nor did the sudden availability of trillions of additional U.S. Dollars result in a general devaluing of our currency against the Euro, Pound or the Yen. Again, to the contrary, the

American Dollar *gained* value, including 50% against the Yen.

This was unexpected. A happy and instructive accident of economic history. A reasonable explanation is that the Great Recession had been caused in part by a reluctance of the Federal Reserve to inject more liquidity to offset the forty year movement of wealth into the hands of the rich – where it mostly just sits.

Liquidity was also lost due to net trade deficits of $18 Trillion since 1992. Over the decades the failure of the Federal Reserve to make up for the lost liquidity being hoarded by the rich or sent overseas to purchase oil and Wal-Mart toys left a huge hole that ultimately contributed to causing the Great Recession. Yet the Federal Reserve failed to act for fear of inflation and currency devaluations similar to what happened in the ten years after the United States went off the gold standard in 1971.

Now, we know better. It may have been an historical accident, but lessons have been learned. We have years of catching up to do. Which all means that we have a powerful tool available to address a number of capital intensive challenges. In addition to an Infrastructure Bank, as discussed previously, the United States could easily establish a Federal

Education Bank to deal with the existing student debt and as a means to finance education going forward.

As its first task, this new financial entity would acquire all existing student debt. All of it. Banks and the Government entities holding the promissory notes would be paid in full, just as in a home refinancing. The Federal Education Bank would then change the terms for those owing the money to provide for interest rates that match the rate available to Wall Street Banks; just as Senator Warren has suggested. That alone would substantially reduce the burden on students.

In addition, a Federal Education Bank could create flexible payment plans that would make repaying student loans as affordable as a cellular phone or cable television bill. No loan forgiveness. The books balance. But a restructuring can make it all work and offer a nice boost to the economy as a whole.

"It is an axiom in my mind that our liberty
Can never be safe but in the hands of the
People themselves, and that, too, of the
People with a certain degree of instruction.
This is the business of the state to effect,
And on a general plan."

Thomas Jefferson

****

QUESTION:

Does the Department of Education Serve a Purpose?

Answer: Yes. It should continue to perform the mission for which it was created.

****

A Better Congress Will:

Resist the continuing efforts to abolish the Department of Education based upon controversies swirling around some of its initiatives.

****

Discussion:

When Congress created the Department of Education in 1979, it declared these purposes:

1. To ensure access to equal educational opportunity for every individual;

2. To supplement and complement the efforts of States, the local school systems and other instrumentalities of the States, the private sector,

public and private educational institutions, public and private nonprofit educational research institutions, community based organizations, parents, and students to improve the quality of education;

3. To encourage the increased involvement of the public, parents, and students in Federal education programs;

4. To promote improvements in the quality and usefulness of education through federally supported research, evaluation, and sharing of information;

5. To improve the coordination of Federal education programs;

6. To improve the management and efficiency of Federal education activities, especially with respect to the process, procedures, and administrative structures for the dispersal of Federal funds, as well as the reduction of unnecessary and duplicative burdens and constraints, including unnecessary paperwork, on the recipients of Federal funds; and

7. To increase the accountability of Federal education programs to the president, the Congress and the public.

Somewhere along the way it became fashionable among the government haters to equate unhappiness with particular programs with the continuing legitimacy of the Department of Education. Dissatisfaction with Common Core somehow is used as an argument to defund or totally abolish the

Department. Particularly on the Republican right, the very existence of the Department is often seen as proof of an over reaching government that seeks to intrude upon the lives of local parents and their school boards.

While those running for the Republican nomination for president routinely use the Department of Education as a punching bag, few take this bombast seriously. It is seen as a necessary pander to the Republican base which becomes unnecessary after the nominee is selected.

Fortunately most agree that all of the reasons that supported the bipartisan creation of the Department still exist.

"There is nothing which can better deserve Our patronage than the promotion of science And literature. Knowledge is in every Country the surest basis of public Happiness."

George Washington

****

QUESTION:

STEM or Humanities – Must we choose?

Answer: Both are essential.

****

A Better Congress Will:

Resist the temptation to discard literature, music, art, social studies, language, and history curriculum in favor of more science, technology, engineering and math (STEM).

****

Discussion:

It seems that at least once a year there is another study released announcing that American children are falling farther behind in the essential business and science studies required for them to compete in an international economy. It is said American jobs go unfilled because our young people lack the fundamental STEM skills. This is why, some argue, we are granting thousands of special need visas to engineers from abroad.

To some the solution is to place greater emphasis on the hard sciences in our schools. Rather than raise taxes to pay for this added commitment it is often argued that limited education budgets require cutting the humanities as an unaffordable luxury. Which, of course, makes perfect sense if one believes that our schools exist purely to feed one dimensional employee candidates to business.

There is no question that the humanities are difficult to score. And this is where we see the lines of the debate. Is there value to a well-rounded educational experience? Do we care whether a student is encouraged to consider literature, history, comparative cultures and the interactions of people over time? Or is it all about calculus and programming?

If funds for education are limited what must be sacrificed? Certainly it seems easiest to lose those courses for which there is no measurable return on investment. But it only seems that way. Unquestionably there is beauty in science and a seductive attractiveness to mathematics. You are right, you are wrong, your score is this or that.

Simple, easy. But a casual willingness to deprive our young people of a greater more expansive educational experience will ultimately cost us the uniquely American characteristic of originality. We need the humanities and STEM; they complement each other.

*"If a doctor, lawyer, or dentist had 40
People in his office at one time, all of whom
Had different needs, and some of whom
Didn't want to be there and were causing
Trouble, and the doctor, lawyer, or dentist,
Without assistance, had to treat them all
With professional excellence for nine
Months, then he might have some conception
Of the classroom teacher's job."*

Donald D. Quinn

****

QUESTION:

*Why Are Some Schools So Much
Better Than Others?*

Answer: This is the essential question and the answer is a combination of location, funding, economic stressors, safety, and taxpayer willingness to fund local schools at a World Class level.

****

A Better Congress Will:

> Set as the policy of the United States a fundamental commitment to all American children that they have access to World Class education through their local schools.

****

Discussion:

K though 12 education has traditionally been a matter of local concern. While Federal resources have always been welcome, the attached strings, not so much. Similarly local officials often bristle at the accountability aspects that too often rest entirely on tests of debatable value. Meanwhile the cost of brick and mortar schools, teachers, updated technology and the other requirements of a modern school pressure local taxpayers to the breaking point.

Blended into this is the Constitutional question associated with faith based and private independent secular schools. Rarely will a parent deny they want the best available education for their child and in many cases they effectively pay twice through school taxes and private tuition. This is simply unfair. We need to resolve these issues instead of incessantly debating them.

A National articulation of our goals is a useful start. If that cannot be accomplished then we should reconsider whether there is a legitimate broader Federal role beyond cash grants designed to help level the playing field with local officials entrusted to use the money effectively. It is time for the investments to show some return, and for those who have been promising so much to take their victory lap – or return to the bench – as the facts speak for themselves.

ARTICLE SEVEN

GOVERNANCE

The Questions:

Majority Rule. Can Congress Handle It?

Is Money Really Speech?

Should There Be Congressional Term Limits?

Voter Identification – Necessary Safeguard of Democracy or Cynical Voter Suppression?

What Constitutional Amendments Would You Support?

What Will You Do After You Leave Congress?

Immigration Reform – How Will You Vote?

Can One Congressman Make a Difference?

"A majority isn't enough; we've got to break A filibuster over there … That's a sad Commentary on where Congress is."
John Podesta

****

QUESTION:

Majority Rule. Can Congress Handle It?

Answer: Yes, the sooner the better.

****

A Better Congress Will:

> ➤ Revise its rules to eliminate all super majorities, filibusters, holds and other parliamentary measures that serve to frustrate the natural and democratic consideration of legislation.

> ➤ Pass and submit to the States for ratification Constitutional Amendments to formally abolish the filibuster and all other super majority vote requirements other than for those few situations where the Constitution itself requires more than a majority.

****

Discussion:

As every fifth grader knows, the United States is not a democracy. Rather, it is a Republic. We do not individually vote on the laws, we elect the people who represent us in Congress to make those votes. So, as a whole, we are a Republic. But within Congress it is, or at least was intended to be, a democracy. And this is what the Constitution intended with Article One establishing the House of Representatives and the Senate.

Plainly the Framers of the Constitution expected that votes in the two chambers would be governed by the obvious principle of majority rule. In fact that is how they ran the Constitutional Convention; each state had one vote and a majority vote won the argument. Even ratification of the Constitution only required the consent of nine of the States to become effective.

In their wisdom these same Framers also envisioned certain select subjects upon which a super majority vote would be required. There are not that many, so here they are, all of the Constitutional exceptions to the principal of majority rule:

Impeachment – two thirds of the Senate

Expulsion of a Member – two thirds vote of the chamber in question

Ratifying a Treaty – two thirds of the Senate

Constitutional Amendments – two thirds of each chamber

That is it. There were just four situations where the Constitution as ratified requires, or even contemplates, a vote requiring more than a majority. Constitutional sticklers can add two more possibilities as contained in the 14th and 25th Amendments. They are:

Eligibility of Confederates to serve – two thirds of each chamber

Removal of a president under disability – two thirds of each chamber

So adding those two we have a total of just six situations where the Constitution, as amended, requires a super-majority. Most will likely agree there are no former Confederates seeking to serve in Congress. So, we are back to just five.

And yet both chambers of Congress have for generations presumed to ignore the Constitution and create a maze of procedures and rules that frustrate anything approaching what the average sensible American would consider a majority rule or democratic environment.

Most egregious is the despised Senate filibuster. Although complicated, the rule currently requires a sixty vote majority in order to move to an actual debate and vote on the pending legislation. Over the years the minority in the Senate, regardless of party, have used their ability to withhold 41 votes as a means to prevent votes on all manner of otherwise popular legislation. For years it was the filibuster that prevented Civil Rights legislation from reaching a vote in the Senate.

From time to time the majority in the Senate threatens what Washington politicos call "the nuclear option". In other words, this threat of "Armageddon" is to vote to revise the rules to require a simple majority. Why this is labeled as such a catastrophic and unthinkable event is a mystery. In 2014, when the Republican/Tea Party coalition Senators withheld confirmation votes on dozens of the President's appointments, believing they could run out the legislative clock, the then Democratic majority finally used a watered down version of the nuclear option to allow confirmations to proceed with less than 60 votes. Dozens of stalled appointments were quickly confirmed. The Nation survived.

Both chambers also routinely adopt rules that place into the hands of the leadership the power to derail proposed legislation through other means of parliamentary maneuvering short of an actual vote. The impact of this is that even legislation which actually commands a bipartisan majority can be prevented from coming to the Floor for a vote. The recent failure of the comprehensive immigration bill is a ready example. The Senate had passed the measure with a comfortable bipartisan majority only to see the Republican/Tea Party coalition leadership refuse to allow a vote in the House.

Thus, by intentional action and design, the two Chambers of Congress operate in a highly undemocratic fashion with the resultant gridlock that we have seen for years. They have rendered themselves incapable of functioning as they were intended.

It is true that the Constitution grants to each chamber the power to determine "rules of its proceedings". For generations this is where the legislative majorities have looked to legitimize procedures that effectively prevent the minority, and even less dominant members of the majority, from moving legislation through. This further explains the poor productivity of the past several Congresses.

An especially appalling demonstration of this was when a freshman Tea Party member of the House of Representatives from Western Pennsylvania took the Floor to denounce the Senate for not acting on all of the bills that the Republican/Tea Party coalition had passed and sent to the Senate for action. Ironically, this cynical rant was being made while the House leadership was blocking a vote on the Senate's immigration reform bill. Not a word, not a peep of complaint was heard from this freshman lawmaker about what was happening in his own chamber.

A Better Congress will grant equal respect to all members and allow bills to proceed in an orderly fashion through to up or down votes. This would reflect the simple and pure philosophy of "one member – one vote". This is what the Constitution, and the People, expect and deserve.

"It's one thing to have a vigorous exchange
Of ideas. But when a select few individuals
And organizations 'own the microphone,' the
Average citizen's voice is effectively drowned
Out by a cacophony of high-priced media
Blitzes."

Olympia Snowe

****

QUESTION:

Is Money Really Speech?

Answer: Unrestricted political money destroys free speech.

****

A Better Congress Will:

Pass and submit to the States a Constitutional Amendment overruling *Citizens United* and allowing Congress to establish campaign finance reforms that can restore a balance to political speech.

****

Discussion:

In an age of over the air and cable television, money purchases access which, in theory, provides all candidates an effective platform for political speech. However, the number of commercial minutes available for such purposes is limited – and

259

expensive. Unlimited political contributions offers those determined to win the opportunity to dominate television, billboards, radio, even social media and thus to swamp the marketplace of ideas with one point of view, or in support of one candidacy or another. If one side purchases all of the channels of communication are they exercising freedom of speech? Or is it something else?

Modern campaign finance law began in 2002, when Congress barely passed the Bipartisan Campaign Reform Act, often called "McCain-Feingold" after the principal sponsors of the law. The law was signed by President Bush. In theory the legislation was intended to curb the influence of political spending through restrictions on how much money an individual could spend, and on what.

With Supreme Court decisions in *Citizens United v Federal Election Commission* (2010) and *McCutchen v Federal Election Commission* (2014), the heart of this campaign reform was destroyed. Individuals, and even corporations and associations, are now free to spend whatever they want with little limitation or control. As the decisions revolved around the supposed equivalence between money and free speech, the Supreme Court, at least as currently constituted, has made it clear that no law can Constitutionally limit the ability of a person (including corporations) to spend as much as they choose to support or oppose any issue or candidate.

Missing from the Courts' analysis is the fact that most of the money devoted to "speech" goes to television and radio advertising. And even with the expansion of cable services there is a limited inventory of commercial time, particularly prime viewership time slots, and the ability to monopolize this time by purchasing blocks in bulk essentially deprives the opposing viewpoint of the same opportunity. If my bullhorn drowns out your bullhorn am I simply exercising free speech? Or am I depriving you of your right to free speech?

There seems little hope that Congress will even try to solve this problem until the amounts expended surpass all reason. We are not there yet. We may see presidential campaigns in the 2016 cycle that approach or exceed Two Billion Dollars each between so called hard money, soft money, and dark money expenditures. It will be a windfall for the political industrial complex of consultants and vendors who service these operations, but a harsh blow to democracy.

Lower down on the ticket, at the Congressional and even state representation level, the money will likewise flow as the political battles are now hand to hand affairs in every part of the Country where polls suggest one side or the other may be vulnerable.

McCain-Feingold passed because at the time the power was perceived to be just about equal on both sides: business on one hand, organized labor on the other. And so both were willing to engage in mutual disarmament negotiations. That balance no longer exists. Having won the class war, the politically active Insatiable Wealthy are going in for the kill. They have been waiting for this chance for a very long time.

To the average voter it may seem hopeless. And it is, unless the public employs its well developed filter to sift out the worst of the noise and invests the time required to dig out the facts leading to an informed decision. In this cause the great leveler is the Internet and social media. Even a starry eyed optimist of a candidate can be seen and heard, often, and in complete sentences, through the Internet.

So there is hope.

"As a lobbyist, I was completely against term Limits, and I know a lot of people are Against term limits, and I was one of the Leaders, because why? As a lobbyist, once You buy a congressional office, you don't Have to re-buy that office in six years, Right?"

Jack Abramof

****

QUESTION:

Should There Be Congressional Term Limits?

Answer: Yes.

****

A Better Congress Will:

Pass and submit to the States for ratification a proposed Amendment limiting any individual's service in Congress to 12 consecutive years in either chamber. Once a former member has been out of Congress for five years they will regain eligibility for another 12 years.

****

Discussion:

As written there were no Constitutional limits on the number of terms or years a representative or senator could serve in Congress. Nor were there limits on how long a president could hold office.

Although Franklin Roosevelt overcame the two term limit tradition set by George Washington, running and winning four times, shortly thereafter Congress passed and the States ratified the 22nd Amendment that included a 10 year, two elected terms, limitation on the president. It is well past time that Congress be held to a similar standard.

It is true that there is some turnover in the House and Senate every two years but incumbents who choose to run for reelection hold their seats 90% of the time. Seniority is king which means those that survive the longest also tend to accumulate power, which reduces the influence of newly elected members. Established representatives also tend to attract donors for their election campaigns and for political action committees that the members use to help solidify their influence.

None of this is healthy and there are few beyond the entrenched leadership of the House and Senate who would argue otherwise. Term limits will assure that there is a healthful diversity of citizens taking their turn representing their neighbors and States in Congress. New leaders will evolve and have incentive to make their mark through positive legislation and reform rather than simply with longevity.

"Men and women in my lifetime have died
Fighting for the right to vote: people like
James Chaney, Andrew Goodman and
Michael Schwerner, who were murdered
While registering black voters in Mississippi
In 1964, and Viola Liuzzo, who was
Murdered by the Ku Klux Klan in 1965
During the Selma march for voting rights."
Jeff Greenfield

****

QUESTION:

Voter Identification – Necessary Safeguard of
Democracy or Simple Voter Suppression?

Answer: Voter suppression.

****

A Better Congress Will:

> Amend the Voting Rights Act to provide for automatic registration of all Americans to vote and to prohibit practices calculated to discourage voting or to make voting more difficult through the calculated selection of polling locations, shortage of ballots or voting machines, or otherwise.

****

Discussion:

Every American should be encouraged to exercise their right to vote and the opportunity to exercise that right should not be impeded or complicated as a matter of political strategy by those who believe that suppressing the vote will enhance their opportunity for electoral victory.

In a rare, and immediately regretted spasm of candor, in 2012 the leader of the Pennsylvania House Republicans celebrated the passage of a voter identification law in the Commonwealth as a path for Mitt Romney to win Pennsylvania's 20 Electoral votes that November, and with them the White House. Of course this was exactly the intent of the legislation as there was no proof of voter fraud sufficient to impose this added inconvenience on the entire population and upon those managing the polls.

Ultimately the Courts of Pennsylvania intervened and all registered Pennsylvanians were free to vote without the chilling requirement of "showing our papers" to local voting officials. The President won the vote in the Commonwealth, as expected, and with it reelection. Following the vote there was no widespread claim of voter misconduct or fraud – despite the absence of voter identification.

It is no accident that the efforts to impede voting tend to be advanced overwhelmingly by Republican politicians in states controlled by Republican legislatures. It is likewise consistently obvious that the purpose of their efforts is to suppress voter turn out based upon an analysis of the impact of such restrictions on groups tending to vote one way or the other. These are the young, the poor, college students, those working multiple jobs, and persons of color.

Of course those arguing in favor of restrictions offer a simple and seductive justification. If a person needs government identification to board an airplane, open a bank account, qualify for government benefits and the like, then why is it so difficult to show the same proof of identity to vote? What is the big deal? Only the niche experts in the field can answer that question but the practical fact is that it does make a difference – or the Republicans would not be bothering.

It is also demonstrated beyond debate that extending the duration of voting serves to increase the number participating in the election. When the days available for voting are reduced the effect is long lines and ultimately the discouragement of many voters trying to squeeze voting in between work, school and family duties. More election machines, and extended voting, is a worthwhile investment in good government. True patriots will do all that they can to encourage their fellow citizens to vote and to make it convenient to do so.

"Instead of giving money to found colleges to Promote learning, why don't they pass a Constitutional amendment prohibiting Anybody from learning anything? If it works As good as the Prohibition one did, why, in Five years we would have the smartest race Of people on earth."

Will Rogers

****

QUESTION:

What Constitutional Amendments Would You Support?

Answer: There are a number of needed reforms to the Constitution in addition to passage of the Equal Rights Amendment, Congressional term limits, election finance reform, and one member one vote reforms in Congress (all discussed elsewhere), that deserve serious consideration. These include: expedited action by the Senate on presidential appointments, and limitations on the length of service for justices of the Supreme Court.

****

A Better Congress Will - Pass and submit to the States for ratification the following:

> ➢ An Amendment requiring the Senate to confirm, or not, all Presidential appointments within sixty days or the nomination shall be deemed approved without a vote.

> ➢ An Amendment limiting the service of a justice of the Supreme Court to fifteen years.

269

Discussion:

In addition to those discussed elsewhere, there are two additional changes to the Constitution that deserve consideration by the States. Adoption of such Amendments requires a two-thirds vote of each chamber of Congress with three-fourths of the States then ratifying.

First, Congress must address the unfortunate trend toward delay in the confirmation of presidential appointments as a means of gaining political leverage. As the presidency or the majority control of the Senate shifts from cycle to cycle otherwise qualified and often distinguished nominees are left in limbo and key vacancies go unfilled. An Amendment requiring an up or down vote within 60 days will end this shabby and undemocratic practice.

This reform, paired with an end to the filibuster, will go far in rehabilitating a Senate that has too often served as a barrier to efficient and responsible government.

Second, the Constitution currently provides that Supreme Court justices shall serve "during good behavior", essentially for life. As a result presidents have taken to appointing relatively young men and women with the expectation that they will serve for thirty years or more and thus project the political leanings of the appointing president into future generations. As a result there is relatively little turn over in the Supreme Court.

Allowing justices to serve for life also has revealed an unfortunate tendency in many instances during the first centuries of our Federal experiment to have justices of advanced age losing, as we all do, our intellectual fast ball. This is reflected, too often, in intemperate language in dissenting opinions and elsewhere which is unbecoming of a justice of the Supreme Court and shakes the confidence of the public in those with the power to overturn laws passed by Congress and signed by an elected president.

Fifteen years of service as a justice will span at least two presidencies and eight Congresses. It will further reasonably assure that every president will have the opportunity to appoint at least one and as many as three Justices. This will also reopen the door to more seasoned candidates as the hope of a thirty year legacy appointment will no longer skew the pool of candidates to younger and less experienced men and women.

These two additional amendments will smooth some of the rough edges of our Constitution.

How has retirement affected my
Golf game? A lot more people beat
Me now."

Dwight D. Eisenhower

****

QUESTION:

What Will You Do After You Leave Congress?

Answer: Something other than become a lobbyist or an executive in an industry affected by my committee duties.

****

A Better Congress Will:

> Disqualify any representative, senator, and senior staff employee from accepting employment as a lobbyist for five years, or the number of years served with Congress, whichever is less.

****

Discussion:

Although members of Congress are well paid compared to the population as a whole, nearly all must bear the expense of maintaining two households and are also generally restricted from other gainful employment while they serve. This partially explains the phenomenon of departing members or key House and Senate employees

273

transitioning to lucrative positions as lobbyists or within industries that were impacted by the actions of committees upon which the legislators or staff served.

Such engagements are not a matter of charity. Either the former member or staffer is being rewarded for their past friendship, or they are being hired for their insider knowledge and access to former colleagues who remain in service to their Country. Both shake the confidence of the American People.

Citizens have the right to know that the decisions being made by their elected representatives are not influenced in the slightest degree by the member's desire to retain the favor of industry in order to assure an easy and profitable transition to the private sector. Similarly, there should be no potential concern that retired members will use their old relationships to gain special access for their clients.

It will be an easy thing for Congress to police itself on this. Legislation should be passed to disqualify any representative, senator, and senior staff employee from accepting employment as a lobbyist for five years, or at least the number of years served with Congress, whichever is less.

In the absence of such prohibitions under law, a candidate for election or reelection to Congress should voluntarily commit absolutely and unconditionally to a five year prohibition from lobbying activities or employment with an industry that was within the jurisdiction of their committees.

"All the problems we face in the United States today can be traced to an unenlightened immigration policy on the part of the American Indian."

Pat Paulsen

****

QUESTION:

Immigration Reform – How Will You Vote?

Answer: Adult individuals who have violated United States law and entered or stayed in the United States without proper authority should be ineligible to become citizens absent pardon or amnesty by the president. However, a sensible program to allow such undocumented visitors to qualify for extended or permanent status must be adopted to resolve the reality of millions of such persons who have become integrated into American society. As for those under 18 years old who accompanied their adult parents into the United States, a path to citizenship should remain open.

****

A Better Congress Will:

> ➤ Adopt laws that set forth a plain and fair pathway granting eligible persons residing in the United States the opportunity to register for extended visitor status with a practical procedure for qualifying for permanent visitor status.

➤ Such laws should include a path for those not yet 18 years of age when they entered the United States to also qualify for citizenship upon performance of designated services or other criteria.

****

Discussion:

According to the Pew Research Center there are about 11.5 Million non-citizen individuals currently residing in the United States without proper legal status. They represent 5.1% of the labor force and over half are from Mexico. With heavy investment in border security and a recession that made work harder to find, this once growing number has stabilized.

In 2013, a healthy bipartisan majority of the Senate passed a comprehensive multipart bill that would have addressed most of the thorny issues the situation presents. President Obama announced that he was prepared to sign the legislation when it was passed by the House of Representatives. It initially appeared that this would happen and all sides would be able to claim success in dealing with the immigration problem.

But there was a hitch. Although there were sufficient votes in the House to pass the measure it would have done so with most members of the

Republican/Tea Party caucus voting against the Bill. In other words, a vote would have resulted in an odd alliance of most Democrats, with just enough Republicans, to pass the measure. With that result Congressional Democrats and the President would have been rightly credited with passage of historic and overdue immigration reform.

This the Republican House leadership could not permit as they had high hopes for winning a greater majority in the House and overtaking the Democrats in the Senate in the November 2014 elections. And so the Republican leadership prevented a vote, and ultimately was rewarded with the greater majority and Senate control. In the history of the United States Congress this ranks as one of the most cynical and calculating abuses of power. Sadly, it was good politics.

It can be reasonably debated whether those who violated the law to enter the United States, or overstayed a lawful entry, should ever be eligible to achieve citizenship. But that is a secondary issue. It is impractical to deport 11.1 million people anywhere and so the principles of practicality and common sense dictate that a path must be found to integrate these millions into the lawful fabric of our Country.

This is especially true for those who were just children when they crossed over the border.

A vigorous debate, followed by a vote, is how Congress was intended to function.

"The purpose of life is not to be happy. It is To be useful, to be honorable, to be Compassionate, to have it make some Difference that you have lived and lived Well."

Ralph Waldo Emerson

****

QUESTION:

What Can One Congressman Do?

Answer: Every member of the House of Representatives represents the same number of citizens and thus has the equal authority, and responsibility, to lead and to follow. A new member should arrive with fresh ideas, prepared to work diligently to build coalitions across party and geographical lines to eliminate gridlock and to do the People's business without regard to the next election.

****

A Better Congress Will:

> ➢ End the procedural obstructions that prevent an individual Congressman from placing before their colleagues legislation deserving of a vote.

> ➢ Prohibit the practice of allowing Members of Congress to immediately seek and accept lucrative employment with business entities and associations regarding which that Member had legislative business or influence during their Congressional service.

> Adopt term limits to end the pattern of concentrating power in Congress into the hands of a few.

****

Discussion:

Given the time and cost involved in gaining a seat to Congress you would think those elected would take it more seriously.

This is especially so in the House of Representatives where each member represents the same number of people and takes the oath with the same authority as their 434 fellow Members. By definition each of these representatives has achieved something remarkable simply by being elected, but getting elected is the easy part. There is substantial collected talent in the Chamber, and yet the result is routinely and consistently disappointing.

Congress, as most organizations, will tend to live up or live down to our expectations. At present the public approval of the performance of Congress ranges from 10% to 20%. A failing grade even on a curve. And yet 90% of the members of Congress running for reelection succeed. It is difficult to imagine any other endeavor or institution where such consistent failure is so assuredly rewarded with another pass at the ball.

And so naturally nothing changes.

But just as naturally there eventually come to the fore leaders unwilling to settle for a mediocre service. They come equipped with vision and a fearlessness that transcends politics and is often inconsistent with the safe path to reelection. A single congressman can lead by example, by diligence, and by a rejection of all ambition to simply get along and go along.

America deserves a Congress it can be proud of, not just one it tolerates. If we want a Better Congress we must start by electing better representatives. One district at a time. And with the clear and unmistakable message to those elected that their future reelection will hinge on performance, not habit.

Acknowledgments

July 4, 2015

This has been a collaborative effort between its principal authors with the assistance of many others who share a vision for a Better Congress and through it a restored America.

Principal among these contributors are Bruce D. Spector, who has delayed his retirement to serve as Campaign Manager and conscience of the Larchuk for a Better Congress campaign, Morgan Jan Larchuk who provided editing help, Julie Ann Sayer who provided research services, Brian Samuel Malkin who has worn many key hats from the earliest days of the Campaign, and "Cousin" Peter N. Georgiades whose commitment to the Constitution sets a standard hard to approach.

Thanks also to Daniel Giza and Megan DeArmit, our two Robert Morris University interns. You are proof young people do care. We do this for you and your generation.

www.ingramcontent.com/pod-product-compliance
Lightning Source LLC
Chambersburg PA
CBHW072115270326
41931CB00010B/1570

9 7 8 0 6 9 2 4 9 4 9 5 0